GOOD NEWS OF GOD

GOOD NEWS OF GOD

*Being Eight Letters
dealing with present problems
and based upon Romans I—VIII*

By

CHARLES E. RAVEN, D.D.

*Master of Christ's College and Regius
Professor of Divinity in the University of Cambridge*

HODDER AND STOUGHTON
LIMITED   LONDON

First printed . . . August, 1943

THIS BOOK IS PRODUCED IN COMPLETE
CONFORMITY WITH THE AUTHORISED
ECONOMY STANDARDS

Made and Printed in Great Britain for
Hodder & Stoughton Limited London by
The Camelot Press Limited
London and Southampton

PREFACE

THESE letters were begun, under a strong sense of urgency, on March 10th, 1943, and written in intervals of end-of-term business and a mission at University College, Bangor, during the next ten days. Then I was laid low with a heart attack, and when the pain had passed my wife let me dictate the concluding portions to her. The scheme of the letters, as will be obvious, is directly derived from the first eight chapters of the Epistle to the Romans. The study of this great gospel first gave me an understanding of Christianity: its exposition has been my constant theme for over thirty years; its relevance, its plain and terrible relevance, to our present situation seems manifest.

For the frankness—some will say the violence—of what follows, there are two reasons.

The first is this sense of urgency.

I have been working for the past three years in as close touch with biologists, botanists and zoologists as with my own theologians. Once again I was impressed by the quality of the scientific outlook; its freedom to grow, sloughing off ideas outworn or disproven; its primary concern for truth and its willingness to stand unreservedly by the verdict of the evidence; its enthusiasm in welcoming novelty and in tracking down elusory data; and in consequence, the kindliness and co-operation of its workers. There is, as I have said elsewhere, shoddy work done by scientists—pretentious, arrogant and even credulous work; but this is only to say that scientists also are human. And if a bit of work is bad, it is very rapidly and generally condemned as such.

Compare this with the position in religion wherein every neophyte, like the sixty anonymous pupils of theological colleges, can pronounce with insolent dogmatism condemnation of principles affirmed by the majority of the bishops, clergy, ministers and laity of South India; or, like the editors of the *Student Movement* or the *Presbyter*, can reject the whole massive achievement of British theological learning as shallow, optimistic, Pelagian and then proceed to replace it by a hotchpotch of second-hand scraps from the Continent; or, like the small but vocal group of Barthians, can set theological over against historical exegesis, and while professing to reject fundamentalism reproduce its most reactionary characteristics, the contrast between religion and science and between piety and social service.

Along with this is the fact that this contrast between the straight thinking of science and the obscurantism of religion is increased by the influence of war. We saw in 1914–18 how under the emotional strain superstitions flourished, young clergy began to pose as "medicine-men," and cheap methods of the sort publicised in *Tell England* gained wide influence. The reaction in Anglicanism then was towards the mediaeval and Catholic: today under similar pressure it seems to be towards continental Protestantism. In both cases the characteristic theology is plainly pathological—but not less dangerous on that account.

Under such circumstances, can one who was brought up in the school of Lightfoot, Hort and Westcott, and was a pupil of H. M. Gwatkin and in some respects of Charles Gore keep silence? *Facit indignatio versum!*

The second reason is my own peculiar status. I have been for thirty-three years in Anglican orders, and have (I imagine and, from Crockford, can indicate) had as wide an experience of varied service as any living theologian. Perhaps on that account I am now entirely without any official status, benefice or other position in the ecclesiastical world—except that my University insisted upon my representing it in Convocation and my friend, the Bishop of

Lichfield, pitying my solitude, has lately made me one of his Examining Chaplains. To my mind, this lack of status is not an excuse for silence, but a constraint to speech. I am that rare thing, an Anglican priest under legal obligation to no bishop and for all practical purposes to no archbishop. I can commit no one by my utterances and can be disowned by all. It ought to be possible, in such happy circumstances, to speak without fear or favour, for God and not for man.

And that is what I have tried to do.

April 1st, 1943. C. E. R.

NOTE.—The letters are addressed to the friend to whom the book, *Science, Religion and the Future*, of which they are the sequel, was dedicated, the Rev. Henry St. John Hart, Dean of Queens' College, Cambridge. This does not make him, or mean that he is, a partaker in my sins.

CONTENTS

I

GOD'S GOSPEL AND OUR NEED

"I am not ashamed of the Gospel." Rom. i. 16

M^Y DEAR HENRY,
    The world—our world of this fourth year of war—
is suffering from locomotor ataxia. The body of mankind
built up and knit together so marvellously by the good
gifts of God in Christian civilisation has failed, hopelessly
failed, to recognise its unity; and so, though physically
integrated by radio and aeroplane, its life is schizophrenic
and its activities consequently unco-ordinated, spasmodic,
meaningless, and self-destructive. I need not cite evidence;
the six million Jews facing extermination; the millions of
Poles, Greeks, Czechs, Belgians and others massacred
or starved; the three million Anglo-American casualties
for whom our strategists are now reputed to be making
ready; the warnings that when this world-war is over,
a third conflict or a military regimentation of mankind
is inescapable. A mad world? A bad world? At least
a world which has lost any sense of direction, any clue
to the meaning of the good life, any power to work
coherently for its achievement. Locomotor ataxia is the
plainest analogy—locomotor ataxia when the sufferer
ceases to be able to control his limbs, or organise his
processes, or express his selfhood—locomotor ataxia, a
condition far more terrible than the death of which it is the
prelude.

If it is true on the large scale, it is, as you and I are
aware, equally true on the small. We see in men who should
be ministers of the Word and teachers of babes only despair
—not the agony of dereliction which can cry, *"Eloi, eloi,*

lama sabachthani" and in that supreme, self-emptying attain fullness of life, but the dull, bewildered futility of an inverted Pharisaism which prides itself on its own damnation, exalts Satan as lord of the earth, and thanks God for "the good news of original sin." It is the despair which, starting from the assumption once so finely voiced by Olive Schreiner that all life is "a striving and a striving and an ending in nothing," empties that confession of its pagan courage, degrades it into a denunciation of all human effort as vanity and illusion, and in the name of Christ proclaims it as a doctrine of total depravity under which presumably it does not matter whether a man behaves like Adolf Hitler or like Mahatma Gandhi. We see the shepherds of Christ's flock—our shepherds of the new or revolutionary theology —persuading their sheep to act like the swine of Gadara, to abandon hope for a world in which God's Kingdom cannot come, and in consequence (being piglike and devil-ridden) to rush down the nearest steep place to destruction and hell. You say well that "a gospel of despair is an oxymoron in theology as it is in grammar": you also say well "but we have not so learned Christ."

It is in this latter conviction that these letters are to be written.

For although I would not impute to you my own errors (if errors they be) or make you partaker of my sins, yet it is plain that to us both the gospel which we hold and are commissioned to proclaim is something vastly different from the prevailing theologies. We see it as still and always good news, as the fulfilment of that "Hope of Catholick Judaism" of which your father wrote, and indeed of that creative process whereto not only Judaism but nature and history bear witness. We see it not as the last, desperate remedy of an otherwise defeated God, nor as a divine (but still desperate) invasion of a world successfully rebellious, nor indeed as in any sense an intrusion *ab extra* of an alien Deity: but as the fulfilment at its appointed season of the loving purpose of the Father, who had in the beginning planned to bring many sons unto glory, and for that end had given His creatures three gifts—freedom and therefore the power to reject; suffering that they might learn the true meaning and use of freedom; and something of His own Spirit to help their infirmities and make fruitful their travail. We rejoice to trace in the long story of evolution the gradual unfolding of His purpose, in human history the closer preparation for the Christ, and in the Biblical records the stirring of the creature in recognition of and response to its God. We rejoice above all to know and declare that in the fullness of time creature and Creator were made one in Jesus, that the perfect Son of Man is also and verily the perfect Son of God, and that the union thus consummated remains for ever, alike as a witness to the true nature of human and divine and as an instrument whereby we may all attain unto the measure of the stature of the Christ.

It has been your chief task to examine with an unsparing use of all the equipment of textual and historical criticism the *testimonia Christi* contained in Scripture. It has been mine to find vaguer but hardly less valuable *testimonia* in wider fields and particularly in the process of creative evolution and the development of human society. Both of us are profoundly conscious of our unfitness for our tasks. You are not less ready than I to acknowledge yourself a chief of sinners. We both confess that in us dwells no good thing save such gift of His Spirit as God in His compassion has granted us. But because we know our own fallen state and grievous need, we are not ready, should indeed passionately refuse, to pronounce God's creation "a sorry piece," to condemn mankind indiscriminately, or to deny that God's will can be done "on earth as it is in heaven." "We have not so learned Christ," and therefore although the days are evil and we may be ashamed of ourselves, we are not ashamed of the Gospel.

For it is, my dear Henry, now as aforetime the power of

God unto salvation. The power of God. When my friend, George Matthai, went from his brilliant career as a zoologist in Cambridge to his professorship at Lahore, happy in his vocation of interpreting Britain to India and India to Britain, and reached his post in time for the Amritsar massacre and the crawling-order in Lahore, and came back a year later a broken man with his life's work smashed before it was begun, it was the power of Christ, experienced afresh during a lonely visit to the Catacombs, that restored him to hope and joy. When my friend, Dick Sheppard, came to me at Ely a few days before his death, choking with asthma and wracked with suffering, so that he could not deliver his speech that evening and could hardly crawl to the Cathedral next morning, it was the power of Christ that kept him radiating courage and cheerfulness for nearly an hour to the hundreds of individuals that spoke to him after the meeting, and sent him back to breakfast chuckling with glee because the Verger had said to him, "You can't come into the Cathedral now; a service is just going to begin." When my friend, the red-haired George Malone, unemployed docker and communist, the lad who after a speech of mine took my arm and walked off with me, saying, "I'm a materialist and you're a Christian, but we agree in everything you've said," it was the power of Christ that sent him to me when his closest friend was ill to say, "I've got a picture—the only thing I've got. My grandad had it. I—well I live by the beauty of it: if it's a real Morland as they told me, it'll be worth money; and I'll have to sell it for my pal. Will you have it valued for me?" Or when my friend, the almost unknown private soldier in the 1st Berkshires, was caught with me under heavy fire on a sunken road in the Cambrai Salient on November 29th, 1917, it was surely the power of Christ that led him to throw his body between me and the shell-bursts, and the face of Christ that he turned to me when, mistaking his movements for fear, I told him to keep still.

Sentimental? Fanciful? Far-fetched? But surely it is out of such stuff that our conviction is formed—out of the myriad acts of self-forgetting goodness done by common folk that we gain our certainty that God is not far off nor has cast off His people, and that mankind is not wholly depraved nor incapable of reflecting His image.

It may be, may it not? though I hesitate to criticise others than myself—it may be that here in academic aloofness from the "profane herd" we do not see enough of human nature to overcome our secret dislike of it. It may be, as the wisest of our present pastors once said in the University pulpit, that "it is easy to be a follower of Dr. Barth if you live in the comfort of a college high table." I do not know. But having mixed pretty freely with men and women of all sorts, and served apprenticeship in half a dozen secular callings, I can only testify that Christ as you and I have known Him is God's power, unconfined by ecclesiastical barriers, manifested to those who have eyes to see and often in unexpected quarters, and amazing us by the authentic quality of love and of much serving. "Raise the stone and thou shalt find Me" is no doubt a logion of doubtful genuineness: neither you nor I would care to guarantee it as an actual word of Jesus. But is it so far from the Lukan utterance, "the Kingdom of God is inside you" (Luke xvii. 21), which was spoken, not to the disciples, but to the Pharisees? Or from the message to St. Peter bidding him to call nothing common or unclean (Acts x. 15, 28)?

You will see, and I believe you will agree with me when you see, that I am following the Apostle not less than the Greek Apologists of the second century, in stressing the universal and inclusive character of the Christ. When St. Paul wrote of Him as "God's mystery in whom are stored all the treasures of wisdom and of knowledge" (Col. ii. 2), he meant more than that Jesus was the Messiah of the Jews or the fulfilment of the Law and the Prophets; but when he also called Him in the same Epistle "the first-born of all creation" (Col. i. 15), he cannot have meant to separate Him off as an alien from the world of nature and humanity. Indeed, as I learnt from your father, when Christ is called "the image of the unseen God" (Col. i. 15) the reference is manifestly to the first chapter of Genesis, and as St. Athanasius afterwards demonstrated (e.g. in *De Incarn.* 3 and *C. Arianos* ii. 78), there is in the two passages the framework of a Christology. Man is created to reflect God like a mirror or bear His image like a coin; sin distorts the reflection or blurs the image; in Jesus the reflection is perfected, the image re-impressed. In either case and in spite of sin, there is a natural congruity between the human and the divine and mankind, even in its fallen state, is still *capax deitatis*, capable of receiving the gift of the oneness of God and man in Christ.

This oneness—which is the plain meaning of the Incarnation—necessarily discloses a valuation of the natural order vastly different from that of the Augustinian, Calvinist and Barthian theologies. It vindicates the language used so unequivocally by St. Irenæus, "He became what we are in order that He might make us become what He is" (*Adv. Haer.*, v. Pref.), and by St. Athanasius, "He became human that we might become divine" (*De Incarn.*, 54, 3). It rules out any Apollinarian, Monophysite or theatrical interpretation of the person of Christ. It affirms the reality and completeness of His manhood not less than the reality and completeness of His Godhead. It is, in fact, the Christology of the New Testament and of the Catholic Creeds, if these are interpreted in their original sense and not as glossed by later concessions to the superstitious. And it is wholly consistent with the Biblical doctrine of the world and of mankind which, though realistic in its acknowledgment of the fact of evil, always regards nature as the scene of God's sovereignty and history as the record of His mighty acts.

Such a belief is compatible alike with the element of truth in scientific humanism—a much larger element than the theology of defeat is ready to admit—and with the due emphasis upon the otherness and energy of God. It is both evolutionary in the sense that it regards the universe as a coherent whole, and its progress as a real development, and catastrophic in its insistence upon the tremendous and trans-forming character of that progress and upon the universality of the law of sacrifice, as the condition of its fulfilment. It does justice to both the essential moments of religious experience, to the exaltation of our communion with God and to the abasement of our penitence before Him. It can give meaning both to the *Te Deum* and to the *Miserere*, to Good Friday and to Easter. Indeed, it insists that these two, the constant antitheses of religion, radically contradictory as they can be made to appear, are yet complementary, mutually indispensable, and ultimately to be synthesised, are indeed perhaps but the obverse and reverse of the divine coinage wherewith God rewards His children. We, like the Apostle, are debtors both to the Greeks and to the Jews, both to those who live naturally in the beauty of His presence and to those whose course is marked by violent convulsions and incessant conflict with evil.

Indeed, for you and me, trained in Cambridge and or-dained in the Church of England, the obligation to Greek and Jew does not present the difficulties upon which so many of our contemporaries insist. We do not find the Greek necessarily optimistic, superficial, morally irrespons-ible, nor the Jew pessimistic, puritanical, sin-obsessed. To us it seems as absurd to interpret Hellenism in terms of Professor Dewey as to interpret Judaism in terms of Pro-fessor Barth. Biblical theology is not to be identified with the morbidities of the North African Fathers; for the religion of Israel in the great prophets, as indeed in the Law and the Writings, is far nearer to the mind and faith of Clement of Alexandria than of Tertullian or St. Augustine; and even the Jewish Apocalytists are not fairly judged when read in the lurid light of the last chapter of the *De*

Spectaculis or even of Dante's *Inferno*. It is the peculiar glory of the Bible that it never mistakes Satan for the successful rival of God nor represents earth as hell. If there are profundities in Jeremiah and St. Paul which cannot be paralleled in Socrates or St. Luke, there is a similar conviction of the worth and meaning of the physical universe as a symbol and instrument of the Eternal, a similar insistence upon the need and possibility of human righteousness, a similar resolve that only as he learns to live eternally does man fulfil his destiny. Thus, when "new theologians" like Dr. Reinhold Niebuhr set Greek and Jew in antithesis, I, scrutinising his treatment of Hellenism, conclude from his many misstatements and loose generalisations that he really knows very little at first hand about it, and you, similarly studying his version of Judaism, comment upon it that he seems to regard Slavonic Enoch as characteristically canonical. Our trouble partly is, my dear Henry, that the new school in theology, like the University of Cambridge in the eighteenth century, is more loyal to its cause than learned in its advocacy.

Our own links are with an earlier and better Cambridge, the Cambridge of the Christian Platonists, of Henry More of Christ's and John Smith of Queens'. It was Henry More, younger contemporary of Milton, pupil of Joseph Mead, friend of Descartes and colleague of Ralph Cudworth, who supplemented the philosophical theology of his *Antidote against Atheism* by the first fully developed appeal to the order of nature as manifesting the character and purpose of God, and who by the influence of this book upon John Ray's *Wisdom of God in the Works of Creation* may well claim to be the ancestor of the whole study of adaptation to environment and the adjustment of structure to function. It was John Smith, pupil of Benjamin Whichcote, and master of theological and of oriental studies, author of the *Select Discourses* which John Worthington collected and edited after his death, who, dying at the age of thirty-four, had already become known as the "living library" and had left a series of utterances which, often the unacknowledged source of the wit and wisdom of Dean Inge, have again defended the case for a reasonable religion. From such men and the great tradition which they enhanced, you and I are proud to claim, however humbly, a direct descent.

Moreover, as Anglicans we can remind the neo-Augustinians and neo-Calvinists of our own day that the greatest evangelist of our church, John Wesley, was also the great opponent of determinism; and that its greatest prophet, Frederick Denison Maurice, the apostle of co-operation, took as his master-principle and impressed upon the whole social movement the concept of human society as a body having many members which he drew from the fourth chapter of the Epistle to the Ephesians. It may be that the Arminianism of Wesley and the Broad Churchmanship of Maurice seem to the "new theology" "blasphemous," "humanistic," "Pelagian." "By their fruits ye shall know them." The Monophysite and Augustinian doctrines in the fifth century were successful in smashing Nestorius and Pelagius: they did not prevent the disruption of the Church, the breakdown of learning and civilisation, the distortion of Christianity into a religion of insurance against hell and escape from the world. They did not prevent—they may even be said to have hastened—the closing in of the Dark Ages. There is no evidence at all, so far as I can see, that their successors in the present day, who claim so arrogantly to be the champions and restorers of orthodoxy, will succeed in doing more than reducing the Church to a few small pietistic and highly factious cliques, obscurantist in their thought, superstitious in their practices, and wholly ineffective in restoring the unity or extending the frontiers of Christendom. You and I would rather err with Wesley and Maurice, with Lightfoot and Hort and Gore and Temple, than err with the *Presbyter* and *Signposts* and the *Church Times*.

I write violently because as you know better than I the times are far too critical and the issues at stake far too serious for anything but plain speaking. The world is suffering from locomotor ataxia and its convulsions are tearing and torturing mankind. Vast numbers of the victims are becoming aware of the situation and are seeking eagerly and not without hope for a remedy. They have at present and in this country two main sources of possible encouragement, the representatives of science and of religion.

They look to the former with a confidence based upon the amazing achievements of the scientific movement in recent times, upon their experience of the honesty and ability of its leaders, and upon their own interest in and understanding of its work. Accounts of the speed and scope of its influence in transforming Russia, even if at first minimised and now exaggerated by propaganda, have made them feel that, with sufficient concentration, if there is courage in experiment, discipline in organisation and ruthlessness in practice, the whole human scene and even the stuff of human nature itself can be reconditioned. Their trust is no doubt vague, ill-informed and often misplaced. Much of it is wishful thinking, derived rather from the romances of Mr. H. G. Wells than from laboratories and breeding stations. But, as the influence of men like Julian Huxley or J. D. Bernal or C. H. Waddington goes to show, there is probably no other field of human activity to which in these days so many people look with confidence. Christian preachers may declare that "Scientific humanism has failed": the phenomenal sales of Dr. Hogben's books and a few minutes' talk with the occupants of any mess or canteen or railway carriage are surely enough to prove that this is not the verdict of the ordinary man.

But there are still those (and they are far more numerous than is commonly supposed) who feel that, excellent as "Science" may be, it does not deal with the things that really matter. To-day, in this age of machinery, there is a new insistence upon the importance of persons and of personal relationships, a dread of the robot, a desire for the emancipation and education and appreciation of mankind. A country which has seen its most cherished possessions disappear as "fuel of fire," and discovered courage and neighbourliness in the furnace, has had to re-examine to some extent at least philosophies and religions. Death alters one's outlook and those who have passed through its shadow carry the mark of it thenceforward. The native desire to know who we are and whither we go becomes a strong constraint. At such times the quest for a religion that shall answer our questions, and give us some promise of security and permanence lays hold even upon those normally earth-bound. If the result is largely an invitation to charlatans and an outcrop of superstitions, it is also an opportunity for all who feel the need to strengthen man's moral and spiritual capabilities. These folk need and deserve help. They turn wistfully to such Christians as they believe to have something to say; and, if they are treated humanly, respond with enthusiasm— until they find the Church, and the Church-goers, and the Church Press! And even then some of them—not so many as of old, but some of them—stay on, and become in due time pillars of the temple.

The camp-followers of science, the camp-followers of religion, do you see any hope at all for the world in either of them? If we take the present trends in both of them, the mildly Marxist humanism of *The Scientific Attitude*, the theology of crisis in *Secular Illusion and Christian Realism*, the prospect seems pretty grim. The message of the very vocal group of younger scientists and scientific journalists seems to have all the defects of communism with none of its human comradeship and infectious vitality: it is doctrinaire, self-conscious, slap-dash and neither scholarly nor spontaneous: it looks too like bourgeois play-acting to be worth much serious consideration. The message of the lions of *Theology* and of the Student Movement—lions "roaring after their prey," but not, I fear, "seeking their meat from God"—has much of the paradox and eloquence of Reinhold Niebuhr, but little of his real passion and sincerity: it is affected, priggish, arrogant, contemptuous of what it does not take the trouble to understand, and apparently incapable of seeing much beyond its own glibly enunciated formulæ; its claims when tested amount to little but ill-digested borrowings from Kierkegaard and Barth, and its assets boil down to a few clichés, "vertical or horizontal," "irruptions into history," "not victory in this world, but vindication at the last day," which sound nice but mean nothing, and to an extensive vocabulary of abuse applied to all who have laboured for critical scholarship, for historical research, for philosophical theology and for a reasonable faith.

"The prophets prophesy falsely and the priests bear rule by their means, and my people love to have it so." Jeremiah's words—those words of terrific indictment—were part of the letter, my dear Henry, with which you launched me upon this correspondence. I believe that you are right—that as with St. Paul when he wrote to the Romans so with us to-day science and religion have alike proved traitors, and we are all under sin, in dire and immediate need, intellectually, morally and spiritually inexcusable, dependent solely upon the divine event in Christ which we have hitherto perverted or denied. There *is* a Gospel, the one Gospel, the fact of Christ. It is, even now, too manifestly effective—in China, India, Uganda, West Africa if not in Britain and America—to be lightly brushed aside. It is, we dare to say, still as of old "the power of God unto salvation unto every one that believeth." But before we look closely at it, we must look first at those rival ideologies of Greek and Jew, of science and religion, which claim to dispense with it or to represent it. What are we to say of them?

Yours ever
CHARLES

II

THE FAILURE OF SCIENCE

"Professing themselves to be wise, they became fools." Rom. i. 22.

MY DEAR HENRY,

It is an irony which future generations will find it hard to believe that this age of ours in which so many dreams of the prophets have been fulfilled should have used those fulfilments, not for the unification of mankind, but for its destruction, not for human excellence, but for human corruption. When Leonardo da Vinci designed his first flying machines, or John Wilkins wrote of his swift and secret messenger, they did so in the belief that the aeroplane and the radio would be instruments of peace and brotherhood; and we have used the one for blitzes and the other for propaganda. *"Capax imperii nisi imperasset"*—Tacitus' epigram might well be the epitaph of scientific humanism. It should have given us heaven; it has, in fact, given us hell.

Why is it? What has gone wrong? Those bewhiskered and benevolent savants whose portraits used to figure on the covers of Rationalist Press Association reprints—T. H. Huxley, and Edward Clodd, and Ingersoll, and Winwood Reade and a dozen others—or even their later and less benevolent successors, did not foresee and certainly did not plan or desire the slaughter-house which their inventions and philosophies have produced. But the fact that they are directly and mainly responsible for it can hardly be denied. Dr. Waddington and his friends may argue that the study of evolution gives us a sufficient basis for human ethics, and that science is therefore adequate as a guide for morals: but the fact remains that the most influential products of science have been the doctrine of the struggle for existence (which T. H. Huxley in his Romanes Lecture accepted as the law of nature and therefore declared that man's efforts must reverse) and with it the glorifying of war in Treitschke, Bernhardi, and our own advocates of ruthlessness and grab down to General Fuller; and the doctrine of the *Herrenvolk* of which Darwin and Galton are the immediate creators, even if Lothrop Stoddard, Houston Chamberlain and the Eugenists are its more reprehensible advocates. Fascism and the rule of rods and axes, Nazism and the dominance of Nordics—these and similar trends derive directly from the *Darwinismus* which supplied the ideas and technique which they express. When my much-honoured teacher, William Bateson, declared it his mission to deliver man from the morality of the Mosaic law and, like a second Lucretius, to dethrone the gods, he certainly did not foresee that his iron determinism ("we are what our gametes are") would sign the death-warrant of Continental Jewry; nor did Pavlov, when he developed his theory of the conditioned reflex, expect that it would produce the "reconditioning" processes of the U.S.S.R. In the last century scientists and their historians used to fulminate against religion for its Inquisition and its wars and its massacres: the parts have been reversed to-day; and science has shown itself at once more ruthless and more efficient in savagery. *The Martyrdom of Man*, when next re-written, will, if its author is honest, have another "villain of the piece."

It is, I think, necessary for us to say this plainly, because so many popular writers—Dr. J. B. S. Haldane being the ablest of them, but Dr. Julian Huxley, Dr. Lancelot Hogben and Mr. J. G. Crowther being the most influential—are pouring out a spate of volumes in which they narrate the history of science, extol the blessings which it has conferred and bid us trust in scientists (or, perhaps, in themselves) to guide us into Utopia. I have drawn attention elsewhere (in my lectures, *Science, Religion and the Future*) to a few of the typical errors of fact and absurdities of argument by which this thesis is accompanied; and if required can specify many more. I do not believe that, as a true rendering of the facts, any competent historian could defend it: I am very sure that the authors whom I have named can only support it by wilfully ignoring the main features of the present situation and by substituting for history a mass of "wishful thinking." I do not dispute the enormous value of science and the scientific method: I do not despair of our being able to use science for the betterment of mankind, indeed as a potent instrument for human welfare: but at present it seems indisputable that it is science (misunderstood perhaps and certainly misapplied) which has promoted and made practicable the enormities of thought and action which have made all previous horrors fade into comparative insignificance. And the blame for this does not rest upon politicians or dictators, but upon those scientists and scientific thinkers who have used their learning to foster degraded and degrading interpretations of man and of the universe.

Look, for a prediction and a parallel, to the tremendous passage (Rom. i. 18–end) in which St. Paul declares the failure of the science of his own day and the terrible consequences that sprang from it.

He, like you and me (though unlike our theologians of the Barthian school), insists that science is a legitimate and precious thing; that, as the Psalmist put it, "the works of the Lord are great, sought out of all them that have pleasure therein" and "worthy to be praised and had in honour"; that, as John Ray would phrase it, "the wisdom of God" ("His eternal power and divinity," Rom. i. 20) is seen "in the works of creation" and that the study of them is "the proper occupation of a Sabbath day." He maintains, as the Old Testament and Judaism generally maintained, that in nature there is a real revelation, and that mankind, if it had followed the true meaning of nature, could have attained fullness of life through it. It is not God nor God's world that is wrong. Man—man's pride and arrogance—is to blame. Science ("thinking himself to be wise," Rom. i. 22) turned his head, and befooled him. Instead of interpreting nature in terms of the highest, he interpreted it in terms of the lowest, of matter, not of mind, of mechanism, not of organism, of the "Life-force," not of the "Holy Spirit." And this is idolatry, and the falsification of standards, and the betrayal of all man's characteristically human attributes, of all man's divinely-inspired potentialities. "They became fools and exchanged the nature of the invisible God for the semblance of the image of corruptible man or bird or beast or creeping thing" (Rom. i. 23). The Apostle had in mind the pagan world of his own day; the words are as true of the materialisms and agnosticisms of the present.

Then, as he points out, comes Nemesis. If man denies his own intuitions of the holy, if he plays the traitor to his supreme inheritance of spiritual sensitiveness and divine revelation, if he bows God out of his world, then the result is not only intellectual sterilisation, but moral depravity. It is surely true that unless the sense of wonder and worship, the experience of the unity and permanence and value of the universe, is given its true place, human relationships lose their worth, and personality becomes an object, not of respect, but of exploitation or of sentimentality. The consequence is a degradation of human relationships at their most intimate and potentially ennobling level. St. Paul sums up the results of the apostasy of science in the indictment with which the passage that I have been quoting ends: "Wherefore, because they had distorted the truth about God into a lie and set the creature above the Creator, God gave them up in their intimate passions to lasciviousness and bodily degradation, to lust and perversion. . . ." And because when sexual life is corrupted, there is an inevitable collapse of all standards, the Apostle finishes with the description of a society in which licentiousness has poisoned the springs of honour and truth so that all the contacts of man with man, social, commercial, civic and religious, are embittered and befouled. It is a story which any honest record of human

24

progress endorses: sex-morals and civilisation rise and fall together; for where there is neither control of one's own passions nor respect for others the basal conditions of a sound corporate life are destroyed. Man relapses into barbarism, using the capacities and inventions of his science for sadism and savagery.

This correlation between a worthy appreciation of the universe, a reverence for human personality, and a high level of public life has not been adequately recognised. There have indeed been far too many who argue that a man's religion has no bearing either upon his private morals or upon his civic conduct, and even that sexual restraints are incompatible with fullness of life or political wisdom. It is not for me, though I was born in Victorian times, to defend puritanism or the ascetic: the taboos and inhibitions of the last century did not produce a widespread chastity and were often hypocritical and obscene. But that a low view of marriage, a contempt for pre-marital restraint, a promiscuity of the kind now occasionally advocated and far too widely practised can contribute to anything but human degradation is, I believe, wholly unsupported by evidence, historical or psychological. It is by schooling in the management of his own passions, by a true, as opposed to a lascivious, understanding of the art of love, and therefore by an increasing reverence for parenthood, the highest of all human functions, that man is fitted and equipped for nobility of achievement in other fields. Education, if it means enabling the pupil to come to full growth, ought to become increasingly concerned with training in right human relationships. For love, which is friendship at its best, is mother not only of the graces, but of the arts. But instead of education in friendships we are nowadays offered education in science —and this usually means specialised gadget-mongering!

Science, as we conceive of it, has failed. St. Paul's diagnosis of the failure of the wisdom of the Greeks seems to me a sufficient account of what has happened. If you treat religion as an illusion and God as a superstition, you will then go on to treat man as a robot and society as a mechanism. Of course, being yourself human, you will not allow other people to treat you in the same way, but your ideas and influence will nevertheless degrade the level of human life and conduct.

You, my dear Henry, will have noticed that in Italy or Southern Ireland or indeed any traditionally Catholic country the usual treatment of animals is revoltingly cruel. It is not that Catholics are otherwise insensitive or sadistic, but that in matters like the blinding of finches in Florence or the driving of cattle in Cork there is a callousness such as even the fox-hunting Englishman rarely displays. This and perhaps their general lack of interest in nature is, I believe, a direct consequence of their belief that animals, having no souls, may be treated harshly without hesitation: cruelty to a beast is as meaningless as cruelty to a bicycle. Similarly, a mechanistic biology or a behaviourist psychology will inevitably lead to the Ogpu and the Gestapo: Trotskyists are vermin, Jews are sub-human; let them be liquidated.

That right ideas do not by themselves make men good is no doubt true. Sin is not merely ignorance; weakness of will remains even when ignorance has been dispelled. But wrong ideas are a fearful obstacle to any progress, and the false philosophies that underlay so much of the scientific movement of the past century have played a very large part in preparing the present disasters.

Unfortunately, as any candid student must admit, the responsibility for those ideas rests not only or chiefly with scientists, but with the religious traditionalists and obscurantists who insisted that discovery must conform to their preconceptions and that any modification of their dogmas was a blasphemy and an atheism. This is a matter on which there is still much misunderstanding; and though I have recently dealt with it in my *Science, Religion and the Future*, you will forgive me if I recapitulate the matter here.

In the early days of science—indeed, right down to the nineteenth century—there was no conflict at all. Individual scientists, like other thinkers, might feel sceptical as to the Christian tradition. But the main motive for the investigation of nature was, as Robert Boyle, the father of chemistry, repeatedly asserted, the deepening of man's knowledge of God. These pioneers, Boyle, Wilkins, Ray, Willughby, Hooke, Grew, Newton, were men of strong and avowed Christian conviction. Not less than Copernicus or Steno, Malpighi or Linnæus, they regarded science as a religious activity to be undertaken reverently and as a means to God's glory. That they found difficulty in reconciling their geology with the novity of the world or the universality of the deluge was a matter which the best of them did not hesitate to acknowledge. But this did not involve hostility or serious perplexity. The tradition was not inerrant, nor the scientific evidence complete.

In the nineteenth century the situation was different. Science was becoming influential: its advocates were challenging the established social order and claiming a place for themselves in education, in government, in the world of wealth and fashion. The work of Tom Paine, that bogy-man of the time of the French Revolution, had driven the upholders of vested interests and of religion into an alliance for mutual protection. The Church of England and to a less extent Christians in general came to identify new ideas with sedition and unbelief; and though in Britain the cleavage between Christianity and social reform was never as absolute as in Catholic countries, Churchmen tended to become reactionary in politics and fundamentalist in theology. Thus when William Buckland wrote his Bridgewater treatise and made of it a valuable survey of the best geological knowledge of the time, it was by his fellow Christians that he was assaulted. "What!" cried Dean Cockburn of York. "Did not God tell Moses how he had made the world? Was God mistaken? Does Professor Buckland know better?" With that sort of argument being used, a conflict was inevitable.

It came to its outbreak over Darwin's book; and its sequel was the truce which confined religion to the world of the unseen and science to its measuring-rods and laboratories. Not only had Christianity become identified with the old Hebrew and inevitably pre-Copernican cosmology, but science had been in effect debarred from any full account of living organisms. The choice for an educated man seemed to lie between mediaevalism and materialism; and as a consequence for all the really important issues in life neither science nor religion gave any effective guidance.

That was almost literally the position in my undergraduate days. Practically every one of the scholars of my own College, and, I think, of the University, was agnostic in outlook and hopelessly confused as to the principles by which personal conduct and social obligation were to be directed. The conspiracy of silence which sustained the prestige of Christianity was still unchallenged except by the few who ventured to expose themselves to the ignominy which attached to the public profession of unbelief. The little groups of genuine Christians were in the main unintelligent—though a few found in the school of Lightfoot, Hort and Westcott, or the social enthusiasm and catholic doctrine of Scott Holland and Gore, or the wider, wiser and more adventurous thinking of James Ward or H. M. Gwatkin a more coherent and satisfying faith. But, even so, for anyone who had a deep concern for biological studies, the first decade of this century was not a time when science and religion walked easily together.

The denial of any possible inheritance of acquired characteristics which followed from Weismann's doctrine of the isolation of the germ-plasm and seemed to make futile all human effort to enlarge the capacities of the race; the insistence upon heredity as the sole factor in determining character which Mendel's experiments established and Bateson's exposition of them applied to psychic as well as physical structure; the

growing suspicion that all mental processes were conditioned by and perhaps mere functions of bodily changes;
the general belief that the universe was a closed system
whose mechanisms would soon be wholly understood;
such claims and beliefs could only have been answered by
philosophers and theologians who had competent knowledge of the data upon which they were based. Yet there
was hardly a single Christian thinker who had ever been
outside the rigidly classical education which still dominated
the public schools or who had ever entered a laboratory or
acquired even the smallest first-hand knowledge of the
natural sciences. The pundits of the Oxford Greats tradition
and the descendents of the Cambridge Biblical scholars
might reaffirm the arguments for Christianity. But they were
men preparing to defend a Norman castle against modern
artillery with the culverins and arquebuses of a bygone age.
Had a resolute attack been delivered, the stronghold would
have gained little from their protection.

In Britain the assault never took place. The two worlds
kept the truce; and contact between them, if slight, remained
generally courteous. On the Continent it was not so: all that
was liberal in education or progressive in politics, all that
looked to the scientific method in its thinking, broke away
from the Christian tradition; accepted doctrines of evolution
and of racialism in an untempered form; and gave birth to
the ideologies, materialist, militarist and Nazi, by which
we are now afflicted.

The Englishman of to-day, my dear Henry, who runs for
his theology to Continental teachers does not realise how
privileged his own country has been in being able to avoid
a head-on collision between science (and all that science
implies) and Christianity. Our young followers of Barth and
Maritain ought to realise the truth which one of the exiled
Louvain professors stated to me in 1915. He was staying at
Emmanuel College and we had been discussing the sights of
Cambridge. "But, my dear Dean," he said to me, "you are

yourself the most surprising thing that I have seen. You are a Christian—though not of my Church; certainly a Christian: and you are a democrat, almost a socialist. That would be impossible in my country." Before we swallow Continental theologies Protestant or Catholic, we should remember that they are formulated by men whose upbringing has been in an atmosphere of acute hostility to any scientific or progressive thought. After all, it is less than twenty years since in the largest Dutch denomination it was heretical not to believe that his ass addressed Balaam in good Hebrew, and for all I know it may be so still—and that in an eminently sensible and socially enlightened country.

The fact is that in our British Churches, in spite of a deep-seated cleavage between science and religion, there was never open war. And in work like that of the Student Movement, the Edinburgh Conference of 1910, the Modern Churchmen's Union in its earlier days, the C.O.P.E.C. movement, and the series of Gifford Lectures there has been real co-operation. Indeed, so far as the intellectual outlook is concerned, if only our theological reactionaries (these loud-voiced champions of a new and Biblical theology) could be given the rebuke which they deserve, the prospect would still be full of promise.

Unfortunately, even here in Britain, the bewilderment and lack of a clear *Weltanschauung* coinciding with a time of very rapid social change—change which particularly affected the relations of the sexes—have done grave harm. The older ones of us, brought up in Victorian reticence and receiving little help from doctors or parsons, accepted the traditional standards, modelled our own behaviour upon them, and had nothing of value to say to a generation in which the emancipation of women and the traffic in contraceptives removed simultaneously the existing safeguards against indulgence. I remember impressing upon every group of Army chaplains who came to our Chaplains' School at St. Omer in 1918 the imperative need for working out a positive defence of Christian ideals and of monogamy, since, as I warned them, the old restraints, chaperonage and the fear of the illegitimate child had disappeared. Plainly the issue was critical. If, as I believed, the partnership of the sexes in the professions and in Parliament was a good thing, and if, as I should also maintain, fear of pregnancy was a rotten motive for chastity, there was now a position in which a real equality between men and women was at last possible. We ought to be on the edge of a new period of frank and wholesome comradeship and co-operation. Humanity could free itself from the chattel theory of womanhood and from the double standard of sex morals and go forward to a richer and healthier marriage and parenthood.

In many cases it has been so. I believe that wiser instruction, more normal and freer friendships between boys and girls, and a less inhibited and obsessed outlook have done much to fulfil our hopes. But neither science nor religion has helped us adequately. There has been much timidity and obscurantism—not least among medical men. Even before the war things were obviously bad: no society that tolerates a practice so æsthetically hideous and sexually obscene as the red-lacquering of finger-nails could possibly be healthy; and when war broke out it was at once evident that we had not built up a positive morality strong enough to stand the strain of mobilisation, with the consequent breaking up of homes, herding of men and women into military units and munition factories, and general demoralisation. It is not for me to assess the extent of the promiscuity and perversion, which is undoubtedly taking place. But if only a fraction of the evidence which comes to us is true, the opportunity of a wholesome sex-life has been lost and a collapse of standards has taken place.

To one like myself who believes that the maintenance of a high level of sexual life is in the long run more important for mankind than any political or economic issue whatsoever, the present failure is a tragic blow. And so long as science has no clear or worthy concept of morality or of religion, so long as it washes its hands of responsibility for the use of its inventions, so long as it calls the study of dead organisms biology and of reflex mechanisms psychology and sneers at metaphysics and theology, there is no sort of prospect that it will help to remedy the evil.

There are signs, thank God, of something better, of an awakening of conscience among many of the younger scientists, and of an insistence by them that they must set their studies in a wider context and pay attention to other and more specifically human subjects of interest. Among the many volumes announcing the excellence of science, past and future, are some which at least recognise that ethics and religion are important elements in human life; that they have played and will continue to play a decisive part in history; and that scientists who wish to contribute to citizenship and social welfare cannot afford to ignore them. The foolish notion, that if only adequate gadgets, good sanitation, medical services, labour-saving devices, a correct vitamin-diet and such-like are provided, man will become not only healthy and wealthy, but wise and righteous, is still surviving, and the present deification of Russia has perhaps contributed to its influence: but the war which science has done so much to exacerbate and so little to assuage, the war which owes so much both in its origin and in its conduct to scientific theories and discoveries, must surely have shaken the naïve belief that mere knowledge can ever bring man peace or remove his proneness to evil.

But what a tale of suffering is required to convince us of our need!

Yours ever
CHARLES

III

THE FAILURE OF RELIGION

"The name of God is blasphemed among the Gentiles through you."
Rom. ii. 24

M<small>Y DEAR</small> H<small>ENRY</small>,

It is easy, as we know, to declare that science has failed, to point the finger of scorn at the claims of humanism as they are illustrated in blitzes and black-outs, in contraceptives for the young and medical murder for the old. That our Hogbens and Crowthers can ignore this plain result of the developments which they so enthusiastically and inaccurately chronicle is proof of the extent to which wishful thinking can go. That they apply the name of science to such propaganda only adds insult to injury.

But it is not for us to point the finger, if we are in any sense speaking in the name of religion. For the retort is too obvious. We are in no position to criticise others when we are ourselves under the same condemnation. Science can at least make the excuse of its youth: it has only been in existence for some three centuries and its influence is not yet fully felt; as it grows to its maturity, mankind will learn to benefit by it. But the Church has had nearly two thousand years of influence, and for sixteen hundred of them has been in a position of unique privilege. That it has done much to preserve civilisation through the ages of barbarism, to foster education, discipline and settled government, and to provide a unifying culture, moral standards and on occasion leadership in discovery may be admitted. Only the prejudiced will wish to deny the contribution made by Christianity to the development of democratic institutions, of individual liberty and of the scientific outlook. But when full acknowledgment has been made, the fact remains that official and organised Christendom has become increasingly reactionary and wholly unable to adapt itself to, let alone to control, the movements which are now transforming (or perhaps destroying) society. Whatever may be said of the worth of the Church in the past, its recent history is one of increasing ineffectiveness, obstructionism and disunity. It is at present negligible in its influence and apparently incapable of standing consistently for the principles that it professes.

I need not press the indictment. These letters would not have been written if it did not seem to me inescapably true. I will merely state in a single instance the clause in it which seems to me most characteristic and most damaging.

In 1924, shortly after my going to Liverpool, I was asked to go down to lunch with one of the most prominent of the younger business men of the city. He had been a colonel in the war—was an influential and very keen member of the Committee responsible for building the new Cathedral—was a partner in a great international banking and trading company—and was a man of keen mind, large experience and progressive outlook. We talked at length and in detail about the chief features of contemporary politics and economics, particularly about the importance of enlisting all possible support for the League of Nations and of bringing pressure upon our own government to make its membership genuine, and about the threats of a general strike and the necessity of bringing miners and mine-owners into a closer relationship. He was very friendly and very well-informed, and we had what Dr. Johnson would have called "good talk." But when I rose to go, he said: "One moment, padre. There's one more thing I must say. *You're a damned fraud.* You come here talking about the need for statesmen to meet in friendship at Geneva, and for masters and men to agree to collaborate in industry. When I see Anglicans and Romans and Presbyterians and Methodists and Congregationalists and Baptists and Unitarians and

Quakers and the Salvation Army and the rest of you Christians meeting and collaborating here in Liverpool, I'll feel that you've some right to expect others to do so. Till then you're a hypocrite—and you know it." I have never seen that that charge was unjust or that there was any answer to it. And the years since then have underlined it. "Ye hypocrites, ye tithe mint and anise and cummin . . . ye lay upon men burdens grievous to be borne . . . and for a pretence make long prayers!" The cap fits exactly.

Play-acting in regard to the relief of suffering, and self-righteousness in its professions of piety, play-acting towards men and self-righteousness towards God—those were the charges which Jesus brought against the Scribes and Pharisees of His own time. They are the charges which are laid against the clergy and ministers, the priests and religious of to-day.

It is our sin against God that is primary, our failure to see Him "to scale" as Christ revealed Him and as nature and history vindicate that revelation. If it is not true that we make God in our own image, at least we have so distorted His likeness with our sentimentalisms, our pietisms, our dogmatisms, our ecclesiasticisms that between the God of the churches and the Jesus of the New Testament there is a crude and obvious contrast. Sentimentalism! We have allowed what my old headmaster called "cursed amiability" to take the place of love, thus eliminating the austerity of the Gospels, blurring the distinction between good and evil and creating a false dilemma over the ruthlessness of nature. God is not a benevolent grandfather giving all the sugar plums to His favourites: on the contrary, He chasteneth every son whom He receiveth, since taking up a cross daily is the condition of discipleship. An ordinand of my acquaintance, stung to remonstrance by a fervid eulogy of "our incomparable liturgy," burst out in my hearing: "Protected against all adversity, may of thee be plenteously rewarded—nearly all the collects ask either for safety or for reward—and

35

we ought to be thinking of adventure and sacrifice." Pietism! Do we really suppose that God is deeply concerned with those niceties of church millinery which fill so much of the interest of the devout; or with the question whether a dying man receives the Eucharist at 11.30 p.m. or 12.5 a.m.; or with the posture in which we pray, or the mode in which we confess our sins? Dogmatism! It was an evil day on which metaphysical subtleties became tests of Christian discipleship: Ulfilas the Arian seems to have been an admirable and most devoted evangelist; and Pelagius to have been morally a better man than St. Augustine. At least these tests were not the conditions which Jesus laid down— "not every one that saith unto me, Lord, Lord"—and the controversies to which they give rise have done and are doing enormous damage to Christendom. Ecclesiasticism! Moral or even doctrinal tests can be defended. Is it seriously urged that the quality of a man's discipleship depends upon the method of appointment of the officers of the denomination to which he belongs—or that the Moderator of the Church of Scotland is necessarily less "divinely instituted" or less fitted to witness and work for God than an Anglican Bishop, or that, in view of the actual facts, the system of Church government is anything but a matter of expediency? If it is seriously argued that manual contact is necessary for the transmission of grace, then let us also admit that the Church is still living in the age of magic. What idea of God can folks have who think these contentions sufficient to justify the divisions of Christendom, who impose them upon natives of Asia and Africa, who, on the score of their ecclesiastical pedigree, thank God that they are holier than these Publicans?

No doubt, my dear Henry, all four of these "isms" have their value. But when large areas of Europe are rejecting the faith, and our own country is rapidly ceasing to be denominationally Christian, it seems time for someone to say, "Proportion, gentlemen, proportion." For the fact is, as recent history has shown, that we can take communion together even if we disagree over profoundly divisive subjects like the inspiration of the Bible or the Christian attitude towards war, but not if one of us belongs to a church that is governed by bishops and the other to one governed by superintendents. This being, I fear, an indication of the mental and practical quality of our discipleship, it is hardly surprising that as leaders of a distracted world the churches cut no ice.

At the present moment it is only the ecclesiastical divisions—the questions of Church order—over which the churches of this country differ. The Edinburgh Conference of 1937 proved that there was no doctrinal disagreement over matters of faith, just as the Oxford Conference of the same year had revealed no disruptive difference in the sphere of "life and work." Moreover, the issues on which the denominational divisions originally arose are to-day almost entirely irrelevant. Our differences, and in their own way they are very sharp, cut clean across church frontiers, so that on all essential matters the progressives in the various communions are in agreement while the Barthians similarly include and unite Anglican, Presbyterian and Independent churchmen. In consequence, in Christian life as (at present) in British politics the official "party-labels" bear little or no relation to actual convictions; and a state of unreality and even confusion is the consequence. Men find themselves divided by frontiers which seem to them artificial and harmful from those with whom they are in the closest sympathy, while brigaded in the public eye at least with others from whom they are poles asunder. Can such a state of insincere and unjustifiable disunion be compatible with a true concept of God or a worthy testimony to him?

It is this failure to see, worship and serve God—it is this failure at the very core of the Church's life—that is responsible for the tragic discrepancies between practice and profession which do far more damage to Christianity than open attacks upon it. Could a church which had any vision of God in Christ have acquiesced, as British churches have done, in the repeated refusal to raise the school leaving age above fourteen—a refusal persisted in for nearly forty years since first the folly and wickedness of the present arrangement was exposed? Could churches, however much corrupted by support of the powers that be, have made no protest against the pronouncement that free competition was the one law of progress and have left it to the Jews, Marx and Engels, to strive for a classless society? Could the servants of Him who condemned salutations in the market place and the chief seats at feasts be really happily represented by one who speaks to them as the "First Citizen in the Empire" or wears the triple crown? When we are solemnly told, as we were recently by a member of the Bench, that the raiment of a modern bishop directly connects the Church of England with the Apostles, we may well feel that nonsense could hardly go further. "Proportion, gentlemen, proportion."

But it is unfair to criticise the great ones of the earth. You and I, or I at any rate, are tarred black with the same slime. A few days ago the head of one of the most effective London settlements, after attending a meeting of "Club," told me how greatly the revolutionary ideas of some of its members had appealed to him. Disestablishment, equalising of incomes for the clergy, abandonment of vicarages and prestige, and all the other current proposals, some of them new to him, if not to us, had been discussed. He came away with a new hope for the church—until, casting an eye on his jersey and corduroys, he murmured, "I somehow wish they hadn't been so perfectly dressed. It doesn't quite fit." Or, to come nearer home still, when my unemployed pal in Liverpool came to talk over my beliefs and principles, and, at the end, said, "If you really feel like that, get out of this and come down to live among us chaps," I know that, being what I am, I could only refuse; and I know that there are excellent reasons for refusing: but, my dear Henry, I have a fairly strong conviction that a better Christian would have acted differently. Do we mean what we preach, or is it just emotion and uplift? We do not see God clearly and so cannot walk straight.

This interdependence of vision and action is of course the basis of all human existence. In this world, and as we believe by our birthright, we experience a relationship and consequent obligations "not of this world." We can only give expression to the heavenly vision in the quite inadequate techniques supplied by life on earth. Some of these derive from primitive, and in these days wholly inappropriate, customs. What justification is there for supposing that because the Jewish priesthood before Christ or the Roman gentry after him wore certain gorgeous dresses, these are still an appropriate method of honouring God? Yet hours of time and reams of paper are devoted to controversies over the cut of a chasuble, and it must be among the hardest tasks of a new bishop to discover when to wear, and how to manage, his mitre. Unhappily, these and similar ceremonialisms are so inextricably confused with religion in the public mind that to suggest that nowadays they belong to museums and art galleries, or, like Santa Claus, to the Christmas bazaar, seems almost a blasphemy. When, my dear Henry, shall we get the thorough and planned research into religious technique which ought to have been the prelude to any proposals for Prayer-book revision?

How deep and destructive are these survivals only becomes apparent as one grows older. Here are two instances. Fifteen years ago, when Francis Underhill and I were addressing schools of clergy up and down the country, we agreed that gaiters and "my-lording" and the consequent itch for "preferment" were destroying the sincerity of many of the clergy; so we pledged one another that if either of us were promoted we would only wear the full dress of the office on occasions on which we would as "inferior clergy" wear frock-coats—that is, for me, at weddings and Royal garden-parties. One week after his appointment to Rochester, he asked to be absolved from the pledge. Incidentally, I never saw him again.

So too with a more famous bishop. He had been my colleague as Examining Chaplain at Llandaff, and we had lived and worked together while starting the Way of Renewal. His appointment to a bishopric was made public when we were together; after giving him my good wishes, I said: "This, I fear, is the end." He answered sadly: "That's the worst of it: you're right." Again, though, I am sure, through no wish of his, a friendship has been abruptly terminated.

Surely these barriers are of the devil's making. It is a dreadful thing to imagine what becomes of the inside of a man when he makes himself a priest and ceases to be a human being. And we, in our theological colleges, are too often seeing it done.

After all these centuries of belief in "the Word made flesh," we still treat religion and life as if they were two things, not one; as if to be good in the religious sense meant something that had no relation to good in conduct in the home, in business, or in the State. I remember arguing with Francis Underhill for many months against his insistence on saying many Offices: I had no secretary and told him that it seemed to me a far more appropriate exercise in Christian prayer to answer my very heavy pile of letters punctually, humanly, and without irritation. After some weeks, I even saw signs of a change in him, though I suppose he, like many clergy, had built his life on the belief that you must give part of your time to God in saying prayers and part to men in giving them help. How we do love to split life up into bits—too often with the result that we say with a sigh of relief, "thank goodness I've said my mattins: now I can get half an hour in the garden before I go to the committee."

And the result is that intolerable hybrid known collectively as "clergy or ministers"!

Honestly, Henry, it seems to me vital to break down this barrier between the sacred and the secular sides of our lives. In a world of officialdom this is, of course, very difficult: but it is worth some sacrifice to preserve one's integrity. Ever since the last war, when I lost nearly all my personal ambitions, I have had a simple rule. If I am offered a job in doing which it would be impossible or improper for me to strip to the waist and wade into a ditch to photograph a bird's nest, I refuse that job. It has saved me once or twice from taking turnings towards positions of dignity. It is hard to escape from our artificial compartments: we must begin by recognising the importance of doing so.

On the intellectual side, this importance bears directly upon our main subject. There is, as we all know, a demand on both sides for "conversations" between representatives of science and of religion. Plainly, closer relations and clearer understanding would be immensely valuable. But few people recognise that there is at present a difficulty to be overcome before discussion can possibly begin—the difficulty presented by the obscurantist or transcendentalist Christian. Nothing is easier than for you or me to join in such discussions. We share the general outlook upon the universe of our scientific friends—that is, we recognise its unity, we affirm the importance both of physical phenomena and of religious experience, and we know that scientists, being, like ourselves, human, do the same. We can start at once with any subject, from the evidence for the existence and nature of God to the place of Christ in our scheme of things or to the relation between evolution and history and the significance of each. Both parties talk the same language and have a common frame of reference. This does not, of course, mean that we and they necessarily agree: plainly, there are large and important problems requiring thorough exploration on which at present typical representatives of our respective subjects differ widely, and in which fuller mutual understanding is urgently desirable. Why not begin the debate?

Because, my dear Henry, as we know only too well, as soon as we begin, there rush in bumbling swarms of "religious" intruders who insist upon "the radical disparity between nature and grace," or "the total otherness of the supernatural" or the infallible authority of Pope, or Church, or Bible, or some other dogma inconsistent with an incarnational philosophy or with common sense or with the facts of the case. We and our scientific friends can only give up our attempts, they (I am afraid) with a sneaking idea that we are either unorthodox or insincere; we with a feeling of helpless and most uncharitable indignation. It is a terrible thing for a theologian to say, but I am forced to say it in all seriousness: the worst enemies of Christian theology—if not indeed of the Christian religion—at the present time are those who identify the faith with ideas belonging inescapably to the pre-scientific world. If, as Christians, we are committed to notions of authority and inspiration, of the supernatural and the sacraments, of the Scriptures and the Creeds, of heaven and hell, of the devil and of Christ—in a word, of the world and man and God—prevalent in those days, then, like the ancient Goth, let us die unbaptised.

For it is not as if these survivals from the age of magic were only held by wild men in Tennessee or "the Protestant underworld." Tribute is paid to them by the leaders of almost every church in Christendom. Official pronouncements are carefully worded so as to be capable of satisfying their champions. From time to time, and notably to-day, they are put forward as necessary elements in Christian orthodoxy. And, my dear Henry, if what you and I and the Archbishop of Canterbury and the Bishop of Birmingham and (I had almost said) all intelligent and modern-minded Christians believe about God is true, then these things are not only false in fact, but radically contradictory of that belief.

The conspiracy of silence which makes such a situation possible, makes impossible any genuine co-operation with scientists and the scientifically minded. It fosters the belief that intelligent Christians know their religion to be an outworn sham, but are concealing their knowledge in the interest of their emoluments and public influence. It allows (and this is its most sinister effect) real hypocrisy on the part of many Christians who deliberately exploit the position.

This is the lie in the soul. When men who know that fundamentalism is absurd and papal infallibility a myth write books talking about the "Word of God" or the "teaching of Holy Church" in a fashion which implies the pre-scientific standpoint, and actually fake evidence against what must be their better judgment, no pretence of "devotion" can excuse the shame of their action. "The prophets prophesy falsely, and the priests bear rule by their means; and my people love to have it so." We have seen in the past few years cases to which that terrible indictment exactly applies. And those who by their silence condone such guilt must carry a share of the blame. They are doing by their acquiescence what Julian, the ablest and most effective of the persecuting emperors, did by deliberate policy: they are doing their uttermost to reduce Christianity to the level of a vulgar and degrading superstition.

There have, of course, been protests. A very honest and very able pupil of mine, a member of our University, is at present in a state of suspension, having notified his bishop and his senior chaplain that he will no longer repeat the clause in the Creed, "He shall come again to judge both the quick and the dead." He argues, rightly as I believe, that this phrase (1) implicitly but clearly denies the living presence of Christ here and now, (2) that it similarly treats judgment as a future, not a present fact, thereby distorting all our ethics, and (3) that it gives the impression that we believe in a literal interpretation of Apocalyptic and a picture of the Second Coming which no one now can accept.

I do not say that this is the particular issue on which I should myself challenge the tradition. But his action at least illustrates how difficult it is for an honest man to work for Christ under the conditions which our cowardice imposes.

Perhaps the most glaring example of our insincerity is furnished by our attitude towards what is loosely called "intercommunion." Ever since 1920 our leaders have professed, and some of them have felt, a deep concern in this matter. Indeed, no one studying the present situation of the several denominations can doubt that "if they do not hang together they will very speedily hang separately." And in the mission field the scandal of our divisions cries aloud. Every competent theologian knows that it is the essential character of a sacrament to be both the symbol of something attained and the instrument towards its fuller attainment. It would appear manifest that the sacrament of unity, ordained in order to deepen the relationship of the disciples with their Lord and with one another, would be universally acknowledged as the proper instrument for all Christians seeking re-union. Instead we profess to seek the Lord's will, "that they all may be one," and repudiate the one means by which that will could effectively be obeyed. Is it surprising that frustration and an atmosphere of make-believe attend our efforts; and that the hope of many grows dim?

In the tremendous denunciation with which St. Paul castigates the religious of his own day—those Jews to whom he belonged and for whom his heart was breaking— there is plain warning for us. If to-day the Christian religion has been disowned by the two greatest Continental powers, if it is identified with the Concordat and Fascism in Italy and with savagery and the repression of all social effort in Spain, if among ourselves the best of our young people, like Samuel Butler, "reject Christ for Christ's sake," and if in consequence Christianity here and in America is coming to be represented only by conventions valuable to vested interests, superstitions surviving from past faith, or fantasies begotten of present despair, the fault lies with ourselves who represent the Church. We are of those to whom it was said, "Ye have made the word of God of none effect by your tradition."

Yours ever

CHARLES

IV

THE GIFT OF FAITH

"Abraham believed God." Rom. iv. 3

MY DEAR HENRY,
    We have looked at failure, our failure, man's failure; and have inferred a need. We cannot, no man can, except he be Lucifer fallen from heaven, the subhuman Giant Despair; or one of those butterfly things (if any such there be) who treat life only as an opportunity for sensuality "eating and drinking, for to-morrow they die"; no man can permanently accept the meaninglessness of the world:

> *"Comes a sunset touch*
> *A fancy from a flower-bell, someone's death,*
> *A chorus-ending from Euripides"*

and acquiescence in failure becomes intolerable: the search begins anew.

What of the search? We who claim to announce good news should have something to say. And now is our moment.

We begin, I think, with simple and elemental things. For man lives not by his cleverness nor by his piety, but by his sensitiveness, by his acceptance of the world and his enjoyment of it and his discovery in it of wonder and of meaning, of value and a presence. We begin where Adam in the old legend began, in a garden. I do not mean, of course, with the Eden of Genesis, and the myth of the apple and the serpent, and the doctrine of the Fall, but with your garden or mine. And if we haven't got a garden, the aspidistra, the window-box, the weed-patch behind the slum, the canal-bank or the railroad or the corner of a field shall take its place.

You remember, I am sure, a great passage in Richard

Jefferies' *Pageant of Summer*, in which by supreme exercise of his power of vision and by the magic of vivid description he makes the corner of a field come alive so that every blade of grass or tuft of rushes strikes home to us as in the moments of our initiation into nature's presence-chamber. You will remember such moments, and in times like these it is good to remember them: they are "the starting-place of prayer," as my friend Claire Sherwood called them; and the recollection recovers for us sanity, and trust, and a child's right of entry into the Kingdom of Heaven.

You have your own moments—*cuique suum sacramentum!* Here are a few of mine.

The first and, as I now see it, the beginning of my consciousness of God, in my first summer term at Uppingham. Three small boys, two Scottish twins and myself, out for a walk on a Sunday afternoon. We had gone down the Leicester road past the mile post, struck left over the fields towards Wardley and the Eye brook; and suddenly—I can see that scene with the inward eye as clearly as the view from my study window now; the fall of the hill, the drift of woodland in all the glory of June across the middle distance, the water meadows and slopes beyond fading into a dim blue haze where earth and sky met and mingled; and close at hand the hedgerow and a red squirrel racing up a little oak, and the blue butterflies dancing over the buttercups. I can see it, and catch the scents of it, and feel the play of wind and sun on my cheek, and experience again the sense of wholeness and goodness, of pulsing and sustaining and integrating life.

Or, again, and this was my coming of age, the day at the end of our summer holiday at Bassenthwaite when I had finished my freshman's year; the day when I set out alone on a bicycle, meaning to go by Keswick and Rosthwaite and Seatoller over the Styehead to Wastdale and back by the coast and Cockermouth, and discovered that the long carry over the pass was too much for me, and felt the pull of

Great Gable, and spent timeless hours on its cairn facing what Ruskin has called the finest view in Europe. I have described that view (*Musings and Memories*, p. 147) and even tried to paint it: but no words nor pigments can tell the wonder of it for a youngster then first initiated into the presence-chamber of the hills and discovering his "Mount of God." I went up a boy, a boy who out of solitariness and great unhappiness was finding joy. I came down a man, ready for a man's adventuring.

The God who walks in the garden in the heat of the day; the God who dwells apart in the high and holy place: so Israel learnt to recollect His presence; so in the childhood of the race and the individual He is disclosed.

But, thank God, the presence so disclosed remains when childhood has passed, remains with growing intensity of appeal and expanding range of impact. How can I select from a hundred moments, which could then be multiplied a hundredfold?

The day in the summer of 1917 in the trenches on the La Bassée front, those old trenches which were a museum full of the mixed evidence of three years of war. I had been gassed—forbidden to do duty, but allowed to hang about in the line. There was a corner of Old-Boots Trench where the naked chalk was bedight with a robe of poppies and corn-flowers and marguerites—the tricolour of France—and where a swallow-tail butterfly and then a big queen hornet thrilled my entomological soul. I sat on the rough revet-ment and made a pencil-sketch of it—the peace of God in a land at war. And down the trench came a stretcher-party and a shapeless bundle that an hour before had been a laughing boy. And the presence enfolded him—plants and insects, the dead and the living were all ablaze with the Shechinah of God.

Or the day in 1927 which was (I suspect) the real birthday of my book, *The Creator Spirit*, the day when the pulling together of my scientific and religious interests was accomplished and I first achieved intellectual integration and a coherent outlook. It was in the Isle of Man on Clay Head overlooking Laxey Bay, where a single rock lies off the coast and a Greater Black-back nesting on it was being mobbed by Herring Gulls, and further off a party of Black Guillemots were courting on the smiling waves. I had been photographing the gulls and making notes of the antics of the auks when again the mystery was enacted. The scene, there as always, remains indelible in my memory. But it was charged with meaning. Hitherto I had exploited nature, collecting pictures and observations, using its resources for the satisfaction of my own curiosity and possessiveness. Now I knew that there was more in it than a playground for the children of men or a training-school for artist or scientist. Here was a world alive, transparent, sacramental; the work of God, the object of His love, the body of His indwelling. It was for me to enjoy. "And God saw that it was good"—that is how its story begins; and "So God loved the world" is the secret of its suffering and its redemption.

Or (and I must bring my recital to an end) the day in 1933 when the collapse of work in which I had spent eight years, the breakdown of friendships, and the sense of helplessness and frustration drove me out to a pursuit which I had forgotten for twenty years, to an evening's moth-collecting in Roswell pits. Lamp, net, treacle-tin, pill-boxes were dug out from their cupboard, and after supper I started off shamefacedly to renew my youth. It was in fact renewed. The eye that can discriminate one species from another—in this case, *Leucania straminea* and *L. obsoleta* from *L. impura*—had not grown dim; the trick of boxing the desired specimen out of a multitude of others on the sugarpatch—a sleight of hand only acquired by years of practice—had not been forgotten: the ancient fascination of that most thrilling hobby resumed its power. But these did nothing but provide a temporary escape. The healing came when

49

with the sudden closing in of darkness the perspective became a silhouette, and the wide horizon of the fenland narrowed down to the small circle of the lamp. You know how in that little world every leaf and reed-blade takes on value; how one becomes aware of ranges of beauty and interest normally ignored. So it was then. But out of the wealth of detail there was for me a drop of water in the axil of a teazle-leaf—a drop of water, and in it all the fullness of God. Our little lives, our fret and pain, so tiny and yet so tremendous. A drop of water and the presence of God.

Those are a few private memories to express the elemental relationship of the individual to God and His world. Remembering them, I am again aware of the parable that more than any other reflects for me this first approach to life, and has haunted me many times. I see myself—and mankind—as a tiny child, just able to walk, exploring a garden in the dusk of a summer's day. The path winds through shrubs, opens up into vistas, closes in, and is overhung with trees. The little footsteps beat and falter and pause; the little heart flutters with fear; tears start into the baby's eyes: for every bush hides a dragon and it is hard to be brave when you are small and alone: panic is not far off. And yet there is in it all a thrill of excitement, and underneath the terror there is trust. The adventure is real and vivid; and lions are abroad after their prey: but the garden is his father's garden and at the end of the path is home. Was it with some such picture in His mind that Jesus said, "Of such is the Kingdom of Heaven"?

It is surely to this basic and elemental confidence that St. Paul appeals when he takes as the starting-point for his exposition of the Gospel the case of Abraham. Back behind the Law, with its sequence of ceremony and ordinance, is the simple fact of God's presence and man's awareness and response. The father of the Hebrews, the hero who heard in a far country the summons to set out in search of "the City that has foundations," was the ancestor and archetype of all the pilgrims whose march is told in the story of nature and of history. He consummates, so to say, the blind groping of the primitive animalcule, seeking it knows not what, and all the ages of life's quest, until so recently the human with its power to perceive its goal and control its road takes over from the beast. He anticipates the generations that are to come, from Moses to Christ, and from Christ to the fulfilment of the journey. And so doing he establishes for us the primary condition of all Creation's striving: we walk by faith, in hope, and, if we will, with love to God reflecting His love to us.

Nor do we walk alone, although in some sense each one of us who follow the road is a pioneer. Our experience, the same experience which makes us aware of the presence of God, opens our eyes also to the fact and value of our fellows. Wordsworth was unnecessarily sentimental when he contrasted the presence "far more deeply interfused, whose dwelling is the light of setting suns" with the presence voiced in "the still, sad music of humanity": for indeed the music is not necessarily still or sad. There was nothing sad about the afternoon in Rabley Copse when my schoolboy son found first one and then another Eyed Hawk moth, and the three of us, my wife and he and I, were caught up into a timeless moment—I have told the story in *Musings and Memories*; or about the evening ten years later when he took me out under the limestone terrace at Ribblehead to see the golden Potentil that he had discovered on his way down from Ingleborough, and we found ourselves sitting below the rock among plants still more precious to us, a patch of Adder's tongue; and he lay back and chuckled; and for me there was all heaven in his laugh.

They crowd in, these memories grave and gay which all have this in common that they echo for me the message of a faith to live by. They link me up with "God and God's children and God's earth" their meeting-place—that is, as you, my dear Henry, have lately reminded us (*Cambridge*

Review, LXIV, p. 175) with the religion of Israel as good Jews accepted and understood it. Recollecting them, I cannot but realise that in fact they form a recurrent motif running through the whole theme of my life and at my best dominating it. My consciousness of the melody varies: sometimes, and for long periods, I am deaf to it; sometimes, even when I listen, discords rush in, and the music is broken and spoiled; but sometimes, and once or twice for months on end, I have heard it continually, and life has moved to its rhythm. And on occasion at critical moments it has rung out strong and clear.

You will know, I am sure, that in this chronicle of small and individual things I am making no sort of claim to special sensitiveness, still less to any "righteousness of mine own." I have simply set down trivial happenings such as make up the lives of every one of us, trivial happenings whose only importance is that they seem to me to be the elemental stuff not only of life, but of religion. I believe that we make a huge mistake when we teach first to our children the immensely difficult lessons of the Creed, or the profound mystery of the Eucharist. We are expecting them to fly before they can run, to run before they can crawl; and for myself I must be content to begin with the alphabet of things.

This, after all, is where Jesus Himself began. To an age which found God in the pomp and splendour of the Temple, and described Him in the catastrophic imagery of the Apocalyptists, He came talking of lilies and birds, sunshine and rain, seedtime and harvest, of fishermen and housewives, farmers and tradesmen. To an age which associated "acts of God" with the unpredictable and the calamitous, He spoke of giving cups of cold water to children and undertaking porterage for a second mile as the marks of discipleship. It is all in keeping with that exaltation of the humble and meek with which His birth was heralded, and with the felon's death by which His work was accomplished. And it is surely at the opposite pole from that scorn of nature as the antithesis of grace, that denunciation of service as mere Pelagianism, which are so familiar in the pulpits of to-day.

The fact is (or so I believe) that life as Jesus and as St. Paul saw it was fundamentally all of a piece. Nothing was common or unclean; the secular was shot through with evidences of God's presence, and would only work properly as it was conformed to His will; and the sacred itself needed redemption, since its righteousness was filthy rags and its splendour wholly dependent upon its power to reflect God. Certainly there is a difference in the extent to which the lily and the child, the cup of cold water and the Eucharist can transmit God: but they are all parts of a sacramental universe and all in their measure symbols and instruments of deity.

As this is to my whole outlook a matter of quite primary importance, you will forgive me if I expatiate upon it. There was a time—twenty years ago now—when my friend, Mrs. Stuart Moore (Evelyn Underhill), had been spending a night with us at Bletchingley Rectory. She was devoted to the Alps and was greatly delighted with a magnificent specimen of the big soldanella which had been brought to me from Chamonix in the previous autumn, had spent the winter under a potted-meat glass, and had sent up no less than seven flower-spikes which at her visit were waving their fringed bells as if in welcome. The plant caused an argument. We both agreed that to us it had a peculiar appeal, and was in a real sense a sacrament, symbolising God and intensifying our awareness of Him. I insisted that between the soldanella and the Elements of the Eucharist there was a wide difference in degree, but no difference in kind. She was equally positive that this was not the case—that the Eucharist was *sui generis* as uniquely associated with Christ. We argued it in a long correspondence—she never quite ready to accept the transubstantiationist miracle which would have given logic to her position, but would, of course, have destroyed any chance of convincing me, and I growing more sure that Browning's lines in *Saul*—

"I but open my eyes,—and perfection, no more and no less,
In the kind I imagined, full-fronts me, and God is seen God
In the star, in the stone, in the flesh, in the soul and the clod"

represent a hierarchy of sacramental media in which the flower and the Elements have each their place. The discussion did me much good: she was a delicious person and as we both agreed to call ourselves "fellow heretics" there was no acrimony in it. But its effect was to expand for me the common definition of the Eucharist as an "extension of the incarnation" until that phrase included in some sense all the universe. "Creation is incarnation" was the sentence with which I concluded our correspondence; and if the Athanasian Creed is orthodoxy, I claim that that aphorism is permissible.

For you will agree, Henry, that it is vital for our whole interpretation of religion that these moments of intense awareness almost amounting to ecstasy with which nature and humanity enrich us should not be written off as spiritually meaningless or Christianly pagan. They seem to me profoundly religious in their quality and influence; thoroughly congruous with the Christian doctrine and experience of God; and fully endorsed by the witness of the Gospels to the teaching of Jesus Christ. Indeed, if I were to be compelled to deny the religious value of flowers and birds and of the natural order, I should find it impossible to believe in the divinity of Christ or in any doctrine of incarnation. If, as I believe, the character of God is "testified to by the things that He has made," if in flower and bird there is some faint reflection of the divine beauty and order and goodness (and who that has seen gentians in Teesdale or a dipper building its nest can doubt it?), if we may find in the story of creative evolution a true "preparation for the Gospel," then it is natural to confess that the fullness of God's self-manifestation to us men has been given in the perfect Son of Man, and that St. Paul's definition of the divine purpose as "to sum up all things in Christ, both things in heaven and things on earth" (Eph. i. 10) has been fulfilled.

But when our critics insist that unless Christ is an alien intruder, "breaking in upon the fallen world from outside", (whatever this jargon means!), then He is not fully divine and therefore not able to save, I can only rub my eyes and wonder how they can so lightheartedly destroy the foundations of the faith. If Christ has nothing in common with us (as they affirm), then we can have no possible criterion by which to appreciate or interpret Him. He remains unintelligible, mythical, from our standpoint monstrous. We cannot use His example; for His life on earth is not that of a man, but of a god pretending to be human: we cannot be moved by His crucifixion; for as the most logical of the Monophysites admitted He counterfeits what He cannot Himself experience: we can only feel that His temptations are a mockery and His passion a stage-play since He is not human, but divine and therefore incapable alike of sin and of suffering. If all that Christianity offers is a myth of a dying god, and membership in a supernatural church, and participation in a magical sacrament, then, on that showing, we have fallen away from the Gospel into the perversion which the fifth century made of it, and Christianity, which, as I believe, in its original form owed nothing to the mystery religions, has become a somewhat refined Mithraism.

"Abraham believed God." St. Paul, faced with the fact that the Law had not saved Israel, but rather so distorted it that it crucified Christ, appeals behind the Law to the primitive religious experience of the ancestor of Judaism. Here was a man who, without any of the later developments of *cultus* or code or creed, had been called the friend of God; a man who had communed with God in the intimacy of his home and pleaded with Him for the forgiveness of his kindred; a man who embodied the simple and unspoiled faith that what God had promised He was also able to perform. If we are to accept the Gospel and bear witness to the power of God, we may well go back behind the distortions and sophistications inaugurated by the reign of Constantine to the faith of the New Testament and to the appreciation of nature and history which it involves and sanctions.

For it is really impossible to be satisfied in these days with the *Weltanschauung* of St. Augustine or of the Scholastics or of the Reformers. The Hebrew outlook upon nature as expressed by the poetry of Genesis or the Psalter is far closer to our own; for it never denies the worth and significance of the world, nor its development and ordered history. The earliest Christian theology, that of the Greek Apologists and of the great doctors of Alexandria, expounded a doctrine of creative and educative evolution whereby the whole story of the universe was treated as the unfolding of a single divine process culminating in the coming of Christ and in the fulfilment of His work. Then came the relapse—I have set out its main causes and features in my book, *The Gospel and the Church*—a relapse which makes the period from the third to the seventeenth century seem with trifling exceptions an irrelevant interlude. It was not until the Biblical and Hellenistic valuation of nature as God's realm and of history as God's acts came again to be accepted, when the scientific movement set itself to see life steadily and see it whole, that any integral and integrative philosophy could be recovered. So long as the natural and the supernatural, the secular and the sacred, the world and the Church, were set out as antitheses, and the former in each case regarded as irrelevant to religion, there could be no science, no social reform, no economic or political effort except such as the Church chose to ignore or was powerless to prevent.

Fortunately, in the last three centuries the love of nature has become so deep-seated a characteristic of our people and we have had so long and fine a succession of teachers who combined scientific knowledge with religious conviction that the present reaction into dualism and superstition can only prevail at the cost of bringing Christianity into complete disrepute. Men and women who have shared the Psalmist's enthusiasm for the works of the Lord and who owe their religious experience to the sort of natural sacraments that I have described will not be convinced of the corruption of nature or the total depravity of man—least of all by preachers whose sincerity is open to doubt. You and I, my dear Henry, have good reason to know how keen and clean are these young naturalists, how honestly they face the issues of life, and how eagerly they discuss and when tested approve the sort of interpretations which we can give. *"Animæ naturaliter Christianæ"*—even Tertullian could not withhold his testimony to the congruity between man's natural intuitions and the Christian faith.

And if we are asked, as we most certainly deserve to be, whether this naturalism of ours has any sort of explanation of the fact of sin or any doctrine of redemption or any deep sense of the value of Christ, then we shall reply that the appeal to Abraham is only the starting-point and not the climax of the story. We have indeed hitherto dealt only with the preparation for the Gospel.

Yours ever

CHARLES

V

THE FACT OF CHRIST

"Christ died for us." Rom. v. 8

My dear Henry,

The faith of Abraham, the faith of the "once-born," belongs normally to the childhood of the race and of the individual. This does not mean that it is to be discarded when "shades of the prison-house begin to close about the growing boy." Indeed, there are some choice and lovely souls (and their existence is a standing disproof of the doctrine of total depravity) who grow up unclouded and free—saints who preserve from childhood their open communion with their Father and find their earthly home what St. Paul described as a "colony of heaven" (Phil. iii. 20). But they are rare: and you and I are not of their number.

For us, as for the majority of humankind, the vision of God is at best broken and spasmodic: we live in a far country and find ample satisfaction in "the husks that the swine did eat"; we are prodigals who have neither the desire nor the power to "arise and go to the Father." We are in fact sinners; and neither our science nor our religion has been able to alter our condition. We are sinners: and the awareness of God that comes to us through nature and mankind is not enough to effect our deliverance. The faith of Abraham needs to be reinforced—indeed, to be transformed—if it is to meet our need.

The position is set out plainly and typically in the poem already quoted, Browning's "Saul," which, with his "Death in the Desert," represents one of the noblest modern interpretations of the faith. The singer in the final outburst of his inspiration cries:

"I have gone the whole round of creation: I saw and I spoke!

. . . . .

I spoke as I saw.
I report, as a man may of God's work—all's love, yet all's law!"

But the announcement, true and precious as it is, has not power enough to—

"Interpose at the difficult minute, snatch Saul the mistake,
Saul the failure, the ruin he seems now,—and bid him awake
From the dream, the probation, the prelude, to find himself set
Clear and safe in new light and new life."

There is nothing in nature or humanity which can break the spell, nothing unless it be the love that suffers. So he pleads to God:

"Would I suffer for him that I love? So would'st Thou—so wilt Thou!

. . . . .

As thy Love is discovered almighty, almighty be proved
Thy power, that exists with and for it, of being Beloved!
He who did most, shall bear most; the strongest shall stand the most weak.
'Tis the weakness in strength that I cry for! my flesh, that I seek
In the Godhead! I seek and I find it. O Saul, it shall be
A Face like my face that receives thee: a Man like to me,
Thou shalt love and be loved by, for ever: a Hand like this hand
Shall throw open the gates of new life to thee! See the Christ stand!"

That represents a poet's interpretation of the new thing which God gave to the world when in the fullness of time the Christ was born. Plainly for us men the sacraments of flower and bird can only convey a limited and preparatory grace—real as we have insisted, but insufficient to reach the whole of our human capabilities for response to the divine.

For, as seems clearly the case, the element in a sacrament which is "the outward and visible sign" can only transmit what falls within its own range; a photograph cannot convey speech nor a gramophone-record form and colour. The same condition which makes each of us susceptible to his own media of communion obviously suggests that for human beings in general the supremely appropriate symbol and instrument will be a human personality. For it is only by the impact of person upon person that the whole of our natures can be influenced. In his earlier and more familiar poem, "An Epistle of Karshish," Browning had expressed this more plainly. After reporting Lazarus' testimony to Jesus as God he concludes:

> *"So, the All-Great were the All-Loving too—*
> *So, through the thunder comes a human voice*
> *Saying, 'O heart I made, a heart beats here!*
> *Face, my hands fashioned, see it in myself!*
> *Thou hast no power nor mayst conceive of mine,*
> *But love I gave thee, with myself to love,*
> *And thou must love me who have died for Thee!'"*

And if the anthropomorphism is too violent for our taste, at least for the Christian it is impossible to interpret the universe in terms which leave Christ's life and work unexplained or to think of God as less loving than Christ.

Of the general principle that for us human beings the only adequate symbol and instrument of God will be a human personality there can surely be no doubt. The *führer-prinzip*, however much we may dislike its present German representative, is unanswerable when it asserts that only as mankind finds its ideals and aspirations embodied in a man, can those ideals become dynamic and transforming. Sun-yat-sen and modern China, Lenin and the Soviets, Mussolini and fascism—without the inspiration of the "Leader," these stupendous revolutions could not have taken place; for their accomplishment depended upon the enthusiasm, the devotion, the confidence which only loyalty to a person can inspire. Love in the full sense and despite Rupert Brooke cannot be given to blankets or even to flags.

If loyalty is focused upon the person of the "leader," it will tend to see him in one significant act, an act which not only illustrates his character, but expresses his achievement. Mithra slaying the bull, Prometheus chained to the rock, Moses with the tablets of the Law, Samson straining at the pillars—these and their like represent the dramatic moment in which the legend reaches its climax and effects our cleansing. It is with a true instinct that St. Paul points to Christ crucified as the consummation of God's gracious gift and the accomplishment of our redemption. In that single event he sees the "mystery," the illuminating and initiatory fact which both unveils the secret of God and thereby admits to a new birth, a moral obligation, and a worshipping fellowship. "We preach Christ crucified," "He died for us"—so the Gospel in its essence is proclaimed.

To us moderns it may well seem remarkable that the Apostle and indeed the New Testament Scriptures in general spend so little time in establishing the historical fact of Jesus Christ, or in proving that He is indeed "come in the flesh." No doubt the need for authentication as the historian of to-day demands it was not then felt—no ancient writer expected or supplied it. No doubt the evidence of eye-witnesses was given more fully in speech than in writings. But whatever the cause for their silence in substantiating it, the fact of the human life of Christ in Galilee and Jerusalem in the early part of our first century is universally taken for granted. Whatever else the writers discuss and differ over, this one thing they all hold in common: that the Gospel is concerned with the man Christ Jesus whom the Jews did to death and whom God raised up. From the earliest creed—in the salutation of the Romans (i. 3, 4)—to the later affirmations in the First or Fourth Gospel, in the Epistle to the Hebrews or the Apocalypse, there is the same basic assumption that this Jesus whom men crucified is Lord and Christ, captain of our salvation and alive for evermore. This is the good news.

In drawing attention to this unanimity and to the proclamation or *kerygma* that expresses it, there is perhaps a danger that we may in our day separate the *kerygma* from the *didache*, the crucial fact of Christ's death from the study of His life, character and teaching which give His death its significance. St. Paul, in the earliest creed, proclaims that Christ was declared to be Son of God with power by the fact of resurrection from the dead, but adds a reference to the holiness of His spirit; and though later in the Epistle he lays sole stress upon His death on behalf of the ungodly it is clear from his insistence upon the imitation of Christ, upon His indwelling in us and our conformity to Him, that he set far more store than his letters usually suggest upon the quality, the words and deeds, of his Master. We need to remember that though it is the death of Christ which explicitly declares the sinfulness of sin, and reveals the forgiving, transforming and unifying love which is its remedy, yet that remedy only becomes effective as we are actually set free from our self-centredness, and come to share the mind of Christ and fulfil His will. If we are to say, "I live, yet not I, Christ lives in me," we must be constantly learning, contemplating and striving to follow His way of life.

Theology has often tended to separate the educative from the redemptive work of Christ, labelling the former Hellenistic and the latter Pauline. It is true that Justin and Clement, stressing the teaching and example of Christ, place their emphasis differently from St. Paul in 1 Corinthians. But St. Athanasius, in his *De Incarnatione*, puts the two lessons side by side; and in fact, if the teaching without the death might leave our wills unconverted, the death without the teaching might equally assume an irrational or even magical significance. We should surely see God's revelation in the whole Christ, even if we recognise that the climax and characteristic event of His ministry is the Cross.

This is the more important at the moment because recent tendencies in critical study have certainly created the impression that we know very little of the authentic utterances of Jesus, that our records have been shaped by oral tradition into conformity with the conventional "forms" of contemporary anecdote, and that though we may accept the bare facts of the Creed or at least the "crucified under Pontius Pilate" as probably historical, the figure of the Saviour cannot any longer be depicted in detail or with much confidence. That this has the effect of assimilating Christianity to a mystery religion, and of replacing the study of the Gospels by devotion to the *cultus*, must not induce us to condemn it without other cause. For whatever we may say of some of the corollaries, the findings of the Form-criticism School have a right to be treated as genuine and honest research. To be exact and ruthless in criticism is the price that we must pay if we are to maintain the historicity of Christ.

I am not fully competent to express an expert opinion upon this recent development of gospel-study, although for many years I worked with Rushbrooke's *Synopticon* as my chief source-book. But, with diffidence, I would put forward the following comments:

(1) That emphasis upon oral tradition is a necessary protest against the exaggerations of an exclusively *literary* criticism: there were too many scholars of a generation ago who behaved as if the New Testament was written in the days of printed books and its authors had possessed all the advantages of modern libraries and works of reference; the hypothesis that the author of the Acts borrowed from Josephus is a good example of the extravagances to which this gave rise.

(2) That nevertheless the indications of sequence and occasion, of graphic and appropriate detail in St. Mark are not consistent with the idea that it is an elaborate arrangement of isolated anecdotes: the case for the Marcan schema

was no doubt overstated—for example, by Burkitt—but it is vastly stronger than Form-criticism or Professor Lightfoot allows.

(3) That questions of dating and authorship cannot be left aside as irrelevant and need not be dismissed as insoluble: the attitude of (for example) *The Riddle of the New Testament* is in this respect disappointing from the standpoint of scholarship and gravely damaging from that of religion: it is not enough to say that certain dogmas were generally held about the year A.D. 70, since Christianity claims to be based upon events which actually happened.

(4) That the quality of the recorded words and deeds of Jesus is radically different from that produced by popular imagination and what Bergson calls *la fonction fabulatrice*: it is as absurd to suppose that a random series of soldiers in the *Grande Armée* could have created the battle orders of Napoleon as to suppose that anonymous disciples in the middle decades of the century created the sayings preserved by the First and Third Evangelists. We know what such imaginative effort did actually give us—the Apocryphal Gospels, Acts and Apocalypses.

It is religiously of the highest importance that this tendency to push the records of the life of our Lord into the background should be arrested. For it is plain fact that it is these records which most of all vindicate the claims made for Him and compel our worship. It is because we have been constrained to say, "Never man spake like this man," or because, when some saying has stabbed us into life, we have cried, "One thing I know, that whereas I was blind now I see," that we are bound in honesty to say also, "My Lord and my God." If to-day as of old the cry of those who are willing to listen to the Churches is, "Sirs, we would see Jesus," it is only from the records of Him that we can satisfy their demand; and it is plain fact that the supreme gift for a preacher or evangelist is to be able to retell with sympathy and vitality these familiar stories so that they come to life and impart life. A Christianity which has lost its hold of the teaching and life of Jesus would have lost its peculiar and distinguishing ethos: it would be without effective content or power to change the stuff and substance of our lives.

That is why, my dear Henry, I am constantly lamenting that no one is doing for us to-day what our friend, Dr. Glover, did for Christendom in the last war by his *Jesus of History*. Whatever critics may say of the academic accuracy of his portrait, it was alive and vitalising; it had something of the secret which drew the multitudes in Galilee and won the devotion of the disciples; it succeeded in "glorifying Jesus." These little books which revive Milton's doctrine of war in heaven, like Mr. C. S. Lewis' *Broadcast Talks*; these gospels of total depravity; these proclamations of judgment and the last day; what power has any one of them, however attractively or violently written, to draw men to Christ—even if it plunges them into despair or bids them flee from the wrath to come or enrols them under the discipline of the Church? And a Christianity without Christ —without the Gospel portraits of the Son of Man—would be (I venture to say) a contradiction in terms. Without the manhood, the words and deeds, of Jesus, even His Cross becomes unmeaning and empty of redemptive efficacy.

But with the portraits to prepare us for the supreme event of Passion and Resurrection, how marvellously that event condenses and consummates all that precedes it! So by this act God meets and interprets, overcomes and enables us to overcome the monstrous evil whereby man crucifies his own true manhood. He reveals this evil, not in its obvious and generally repudiated forms only, but as infecting and perverting man's best achievements, human culture in the Sadducees, human justice in Pilate, human piety in the Pharisees, human discipleship in Judas. He reveals it in its effects—the working out of it in the suffering and destruction of the innocent. He reveals it as He draws it upon

Himself, takes its impact, and by the love that forgives and endures and sacrifices to the uttermost, brings at last good out of it. Then when He and His followers have alike passed through a hell of dereliction and seeming defeat comes victory, and an indestructible communion, and release for fullness of life and service. They and He become one in the fellowship, the indwelling and energising presence of His Spirit, at Pentecost, and can go out to bear witness to all nations.

I have spoken, as you will see, of the Passion as an act of God; and this is, I believe, the answer which it compels one to give to the questions: Who, then, is this? What think ye of Christ? Previously men had depicted divinity in hymns like Homer or statues like Pheidias or tragic drama like Æschylus in the *Prometheus* and Euripides in the *Alcestis*; or had discussed it like Cicero in the *De Natura Deorum*, or the author of the Book of Job; or had shown us glimpses of it in their own divine deeds, like Socrates discharging with his last breath his debt to Æsculapius or Jeremiah pronouncing judgment upon the king at peril of his life. Here was One whose revelation was more immediate and complete; One in whom a thing new, unpredictable and perfect had emerged; One in whose words and deeds men saw an originality and mastery (Matt. vii. 29; Mark i. 27) which attracted their admiration, perplexed and then illuminated their understanding (Mark vi. 2, viii. 29) and filled them with a new and seemingly limitless consciousness of the reality and presence of God. It was not that from His divine words of poetry and wisdom or from His divine deeds of help and healing they learnt new ideas about God: but that in Jesus Himself so speaking and acting they found the perfect object of their adoration. What sunset and flower-bell, prophet and saint had done at the appropriate level and in part, this Jesus did with a transcendent completeness that not only fulfilled and surpassed all their expectations, but opened up for them unending vistas beyond the limits of

66

their apprehension. In Him all things were made new for them, in Him as the object alike of their devotion and of their imitation they had found integration of personality, power for service and an outlook which could face life and death with confidence and joy.

But if we answer the question by the confession of His Godhead, it must be made clear (as the language of the last paragraph has made it clear to those who read it carefully) that this does not involve any denial of His full manhood or any acceptance of the crude and essentially pagan anthropomorphism which is so commonly employed by popular and amateur theologians. The myth of the sons of the gods who came down from heaven in order to take part in the loves or wars of men is common to Genesis (vi. 2) and to the *Iliad*; and Milton employed the same imagery almost to the verge of the ridiculous in his account of the Satanic artillery in *Paradise Lost* (vii. 469–605). Such language may be permissible in legend and poetry: it would be pedantic to object to it if used with reasonable dignity in hymns and prayers. But in theology or expositions of the faith which are meant to be accurate it is surely altogether out of place. When, for instance, Mr. C. S. Lewis (in an article in *Think*, No. 1) writes, "He became a man to mend you (how would you like to become a cow for several years?)," he is suggesting that God became a man as Jupiter in the legend of Europa became a bull; that God is a sort of Proteus; and that Christianity belongs to the stage of civilisation in which masquerading deities were taken seriously. It may be necessary to keep and employ some of the pre-Copernican terms which come to us in Scripture or the Creeds. But large numbers of our people still take such local and spatial metaphors literally, assuming, like the Black Rubric, that Christ's "natural" body is still sitting on a throne somewhere "above the bright blue sky," and as a result repudiate Christianity altogether when they discover that the cosmology and astronomy with which such words associate it can no longer be believed. They do so in their hundreds.

That such language suggests that Christianity is out of date is good enough reason for its rejection. More serious, I believe, is its effect in producing a false picture of God in more learned circles. When my scientific friends tell me that they cannot believe in a personal Deity, I generally discover that what they mean by that term is a God individual in His characteristics, changeable in His operations, "a person" in the sense in which the title is applied to a human being. Their picture of Him is coloured partly by the more naïve utterances of the Old Testament, partly by recollection of pre-Reformation Trinity brasses and of Blake's illustrations of Job, but mainly by language about the sending and descent of Christ such as we have been condemning. They do not mean (nor I fancy does Professor Whitehead in the famous passage in *Religion in the Making*, pp. 58–67) to affirm that God is impersonal, a blind force, a mechanical first-cause; and when I use the term "superpersonal," which I prefer to "personal" simply because it prevents "personal" from being identified with "individual," they generally agree that this is satisfactory to them. But the crude anthropomorphic and often tritheistic language of popular theology creates a belief that Christianity is incurably mythological and childish; and the violent attacks by the Church Press on all of us who are trying to alter this language into something more intelligible and incidentally more orthodox underline the conviction that we are trying to bolster up an anachronism.

In this connection, it is, of course, a real misfortune that in our version of Trinitarian doctrine the Latin word *persona* should have replaced the Greek *hypostasis*. That *persona* never meant what we now mean by "person" is obvious to any who remembers that *Dramatis personæ* means the characters or parts in a play. But when translated into "person" the term naturally takes on the meaning of an individual centre of consciousness, which suggests that the doctrine is really one of three gods united in a sort of family partnership. And however attractive this picture may be, it is very certainly one which St. Athanasius and all the contemporary champions of the Nicene Creed, Greek or Latin, would have repudiated with horror.

I have passed, my dear Henry, from the very heart of our Christian experience, the mystery contained in the words, "Christ died for us," to theological niceties—as they may seem to some. To me, as I believe to you, it is essential that Christ and His sacrifice should be regarded both as the representative and climax of the creative process and at the same time as the initiator and sustainer of the new age. To estrange Him from nature and history, to give to Him the character of an alien invader, to make of His manhood a disguise and of His temptations a sham fight, this is to empty His revelation of its power to reveal and to reduce His incarnation to the level of previous and mythical theophanies. Unless our theological language is used more exactly and more accurately, the impression that Christianity is "a creed outworn" will remain and very rapidly increase. No doubt the Christian experience will survive even under those conditions: but it will be terribly hard for honest modern minds to accept it; and it will become (even more than it is to-day) an escape for those who cannot face reality.

Yours ever

CHARLES

VI

THE CONQUEST OF EVIL

"Dead indeed unto sin but alive unto God." Rom. vi. 11

My dear Henry,

There are, I suppose, moments, many and long, in the lives of us all when the claims made by Christians on their own behalf, if not on behalf of Christ, seem ridiculously exaggerated. I remember listening in my youth to a dear Evangelical parson explaining the doctrine of assurance—telling us how and why he knew himself to be saved. He was an excellent man—of that I had no doubt: but, like the rest of us, he had his little faults, a slightly sharp temper with his juniors, a somewhat too conscious rectitude towards the world in general, a manner as of "sugar and spice and all things nice" to his friends: and I could not believe that he was not fretted by doubts as to the compatibility of these faults with the certainty of salvation. Was he really satisfied of his discipleship? And if so was not his complacency a proof of damnation? "I thank Thee, God, that I am not as other men are"—how could any of us come into the presence except on the sole ground of our need for forgiveness? I wondered then; and I wonder still.

For myself there were, so far as I can judge, three stages in my return to faith after the smashing of my childish and adolescent religion; and they are relevant to this matter of the effect of Christ upon the believer.

There was first the establishing of the historical evidence for the fact of Christ. Scripture was obviously not infallible, whatever Roman Catholics and Fundamentalists might say. Adam and Eve, Noah and the Ark, Balaam and his ass, these and much else were plain mythology—fascinating, and as compared with parallel stories in other traditions, seemly and edifying, but not to be received as factually true without the slaughter of one's intellectual honesty. If faith meant credulity, then one must die an infidel. There have been occasions when the faith of French charcoal-burner or Irish peasant seemed enviable—occasions too when I should love to dance to a barrel-organ or believe in Father Christmas: but Christ's blessing upon children did not imply that arrested development and deliberate ignorance were conditions of discipleship. And if not, and if one were given curiosity and intelligence and the power to learn and study and think, and if, as He is said to have claimed, Christ is the truth, God's truth, then this business of scholarship is essential. It is not, of course, a task that is ever complete. New evidence, for or against; new emphases and interpretations; and, for one's own growth, if not for the sake of the subject, a constant need to revise and repeat; the process, sometimes painful when cherished beliefs have to be abandoned, sometimes exhilarating when intuitions and hopes find unexpected vindication, always of absorbing interest because always there are fresh discoveries, is part of our Christian duty.

Secondly, when the fact of Christ's objective and historical existence became probable, there was the question of His influence. He had plainly changed human history and transformed many lives. Men ascribed to Him sudden conversions like that of Saul of Tarsus, or gradual empowering like that of Simon Peter. They spoke of faith and its efficacy, of redemption and salvation, of the Atonement as the consequence of the Incarnation. What did this actually mean? How did the influence work? Was it just superstition and suggestion? Or was there ground for maintaining that it was psychologically intelligible and rationally arguable? In my own case, these questions were wholly unanswered—I believed faith to be gullibility, and conversion a collapse into unreason, and discipleship a "matter of words and names" and self-delusion—until I was set down to read under constraint the Epistle to the Romans. Then certain facts became plain—that the author was both brilliantly able and intellectually honest; that, given the fact of Christ, acceptance of that fact would produce the effects here ascribed to it; that therefore there was a *prima facie* case for the validity of the experience. The words used to describe it which had seemed mere jargon became significant and appropriate. Here was a real man describing real things.

Thirdly, and this only happened after these two preliminaries had been explored, the realisation suddenly came to me that the existence of Christ and His influence upon men were not only a theoretical possibility, but an actual and experienced fact. I was myself "converted"—the old term is alone fit to describe what happened; and the process of transformation, studied in St. Paul's case, began to take place in me. A vivid consciousness of the living presence of Christ, an intense and releasing devotion to Him, a feeling that the whole world had become new, a resolve to let this experience control all my activities, a desire to share it with others—no doubt it followed a familiar pattern and has been discussed a hundred times by students of conversion: but the glory of it remains, and even now, as an old man, I am more sure of it as a thing not only real in itself but abiding and most effective in its results than I am of any other event in my life.

And this, my dear Henry, is I suppose something at least of what assurance means. "I know Him whom I have believed" (2 Tim. i. 12), "To me to live is Christ" (Phil. i. 21), "Christ, the same yesterday, to-day and for ever" (Heb. xiii. 8). I have no right to accept those words: but I can't help doing so. However much I deny them, and forget and forsake, they are at bottom the thing that I hold most certain, the thing that has remained with me when death seemed only a matter of seconds, the thing that gives meaning and worth, a centre and a direction, to all else.

Yet for me this does not carry any particular confidence as to my own destiny, still less as to my own worth. There are "seasons of refreshing," not only on spring mornings when life seems "good and gay," but at other times when the fret of ambition, and the irritation of always having too much to do, and the dislike of certain folks disappear and one can forget about oneself and live in the love of God and one's neighbour. At such times God seems very near, sometimes in Christ and sometimes in people and things; and one gets a glimpse of what open vision or living in the presence of the invisible means. But these are still only the mountain-tops of life; and for the most part there is only the old sense of miserable egoisms, missed opportunities, tasks too hard, obligations too exacting, and a knowledge that though God and His Christ stand sure I am inescapably committed to the far country and its pigs. It is a depressing business—depressing even in the daytime—and in the small hours when every neglected duty rises up in judgment and every hope and effort turns to frustration and shame it is dereliction and hell. And the doctrine of assurance gives no comfort—indeed, rather the reverse; for it is just one's own selfhood with its pride and its morbidity, its exaltations and agonies, that one wants to be rid of. If salvation means deliverance from self, I haven't got it; and if it doesn't, I don't (at present) want it.

Yet as I read the chapters which first gave me an idea of what the Christian experience meant and to which at every growing-point of my life since then I have returned, it seems to me at least doubtful whether even the Apostle found the new life in Christ so immediate and final as at first it appeared. You will have noticed the succession of metaphors with which he seeks to express the effects of Christ's work.

First, it is the metaphor of death and life, of death with Christ and resurrection with Him. This springs naturally out of the experience of self-identification with Christ which is increasingly the master-motif of St. Paul's thought, from

F   73

its first utterances in the "I live; yet not I" of Galatians (ii. 20) to the "Till we all attain" of Ephesians (iv. 13). It marks the finality of the act of redemption that "the old things have passed away and all things are become new" (2 Cor. v. 17) in an event as irrevocable as the grave. Man, even the most ill-qualified convert, cannot continue in sin; for he is dead to it in Christ. So it should be: but is it? Has the change been in fact so final?

So he tries another metaphor, the familiar fact of slavery. Sin is an enslavement, a tyranny, under which mankind is helpless. But now the strong man has been dispossessed: the Lord Christ has stripped him of his power and released his slaves. They have passed over to a new master, and in loyalty to their deliverer can no longer dally with evil. The change is not as final as death, nor as automatic in its operation: it is now conditioned by the loyalty of the slave to his new owner.

Even this does not do justice to the facts. Christ is no tyrant, nor does He treat His disciples as slaves. "I have called you my friends" (John xv. 15) is a conviction cardinal to St. Paul's belief. So a third metaphor is introduced, that of the most intimate of all human relationships, marriage. The Apostle was later to work out the imagery in relation to the Church, and give us the symbolism of the bride of Christ with all that this has meant for the devotional life. But here he contents himself with a simpler treatment. The disciple is not bound to Christ as a slave to his master, not bound by external compulsion and the power of force, but as a wife to her husband by the ties of affection and mutual obligation, so that it is a betrayal and an adultery to break the pact. Now that the old partnership with evil is finished, and the new marriage has been contracted, there can be no hankering after the shame of the past.

So he pleads, urging the completeness of the deliverance, and the impossibility of going back upon it, insisting that sin has been defeated and slain, that the new life is available and has been accepted, and that it is monstrous, a madness and a folly, to continue in the old. He pleads; and his argument is impressive, almost indeed irresistible. We feel that in view of what Christ is and has done there can be no half-hearted acceptance, no room for any other interest or concern, no return to the things in which we had found no satisfaction, but only futility and shame. It seems a clearly established contention.

Nonetheless, the doubt persists. Christ is victor: of that there is no question. Man's age-old entail of inherited taint, man's persistent and helpless bondage to pride and greed, to lust and enmity, man's estrangement from God—these are at an end. Life is not, cannot ever again be, "a striving and a striving and an ending in nothing": Adam's curse is done away: the Fall, however that terrible fact is interpreted, no longer involves us: Christ lives and reigns.

But do things work out quite so simply? Is the power of sin so obsolete in fact as it should be in doctrine? Does the Gospel achieve so immediate and so easy a deliverance? The lives of these converts do not seem to verify such a conclusion. Changed they certainly are: witness the miracle at Corinth, where in a city synonymous with commercialised vice and religious prostitution it had been possible to sing of "the more excellent way" in the praise of "faith, hope, love, these three." There was a radiance in their faces, a purpose in their lives, a power in their community wholly new and splendidly reassuring. But there were scandals. The way was not all smooth and simple. To follow it was not an effortless descent: parts of it were arduous, some of it was almost cruelly hard. If there was always the company and encouragement of Him who had gone before, and always the view of a wide horizon, yet to walk with Christ demanded vigilance and energy, and at times neither companion nor goal was clearly seen.

Even in himself, the Apostle, it was not certain that the metaphors really fitted the facts. If he were deadly honest, if he were ready to strip and expose his own intimate life, could he say that it was sinless? Was it true, even of him, that to see was to act? That he had the mind of Christ and could without hesitation or struggle put that mind into effect? Was he, Paul, so perfectly at one with God as to be wholly and inevitably free from sin? There could be only one answer to such questions.

Commentators, both the predestinarians, who cannot admit that the elect are not straightway sanctified, and the pietists, who must exaggerate the miraculous consequences of conversion, have made nonsense of the Apostle's argument, and incidentally have depreciated one of the most valiant of his heroisms, by insisting that in the poignant lines in which he discloses his own inward strivings and bitter consciousness of need he is writing of things remembered from his pre-Christian past—that the Paul who confessed, "I see another law in my members campaigning against the law of my mind and bringing me into captivity," was recollecting a mood of his unconverted life—that the cry "Miserable man that I am, who shall redeem me from the body of this death" was not the utterance of a heart perpetually broken by its own helplessness, but a theatrical and vicarious expression on behalf of his would-be followers. So do commentators empty of its meaning the dereliction of the Crucified!

Surely, as any honest and intelligent exegesis must admit, and as anyone who follows his interpretation of Christ's religion will joyfully maintain, we have here the expression of stark truth, and an analysis of religious experience of supreme value. After the metaphors, so significant and yet so insufficient, here is confession, the frank unveiling of the secret agony at the core of his own seemingly triumphant achievement. He, Paul the dauntless, Paul whose new name proves that he has died with Christ, Paul the bond-slave of Jesus, is still a man in whose will is a divided loyalty. He knows what he ought to do: he knows it, and approves it, and intends it. And yet in him also, as in the rest of us, there is the ugly fact of sin; and "the evil that I would not that I do." The strife is not over: it continues. The goal is not reached: it remains ahead. Life is not the sequel of a victory without a morrow: it still demands the uttermost of effort and endurance, of penitence and loyalty.

So by the courage of his confession he accomplishes what could not be given to us at lesser cost. Here at last is defined the thing that Christ has done. He has not gained for us a career of automatic sinlessness, or admitted us to a lotus-land of ease and security. He has not taken from us our obligation to effort or the reality of our conflicts; they remain and are intensified. He has indeed conquered Satan and set up God's reign upon earth: but neither conquest nor kingdom can be ours unearned, and the price is still the same "whoso loveth his life loseth it, whoso loseth it for my sake. . . ." He has shown us the way by following it Himself to its end; and He is ready to accompany us as we tread it: but there is no short-cut, no miraculous removing of the obstacles, no lessening of the need for fortitude, no guarantee that we shall not fail.

No guarantee? Perhaps not: for success is never mechanical or irrevocably assured. But there is a hope and a promise, and the certainty that Christ will not fail us, and that resources, the infinite resources and compassion of God, are available for our use. There, in God, is our assurance. Our confidence must express itself, not in the claim, which can perhaps never be free from arrogance, that "I am saved," but in the affirmation, "Jesus Christ is Saviour and I am His." "In Christ"—that, as St. Paul came to maintain more and more emphatically, is the governing condition of the new life: "in Christ"—so by His indwelling, so by our love responding to Him, we are refashioned.

Here, so far as I can dare to judge, the Apostle "speaks to our condition." He does not offer to us a perfection which we cannot reach without ceasing to be human, a perfection

77

which if it meant the honeyed bliss that some have ascribed to the Beatific Vision would be rejected by our best selves as it is in Sorley's Gifford lectures, or as William James rejected the prospect of a perpetual Chautauqua. He does not pretend that now the vanishing trick has been played and evil has disappeared and we can proceed to behave like angels. Those of us who have reached any sort of maturity would not believe him if he did; for we have ceased to enjoy the dream of a heaven in terms of "Jerusalem the golden" or to believe that the scarred warriors of the Cross "for ever and for ever are clad in robes of white." We are convinced that, as a doctor friend of mine who had suffered and seen suffering put it, "if there were no suffering, there would be no forgiveness and no sympathy, and life would lose its value." Whatever may be the case hereafter, our virtue is in the conflict and not in the victory.

That is, to me at least, true. Some day, in the fullness and completing of time, evil will be done away, but surely not, even then, the activity of self-giving. Love and much serving seem to me the essentials of creativity—that is of the life of God; and if so, even Paradise can never be passive or complacent; even in heaven there will be

> "*the tension thrills*
> *Of that supreme endeavour*
> *Which gives to God for ever and for ever*
> *A joy that is more ancient than the hills.*"

But while this is granted, yet the fact remains that in Christ all things, the whole quality of this life of conflict, are made new. It makes the whole difference that in Him we know and see and can experience what life really is. Previously, though prophets and poets gave us their vision of life triumphant, whether in terms of the garden of Eden before the Fall or of the Sion of the redeemed, when "the earth shall be filled with the glory of God," there was no certainty as to the character of the dream or the means of its fulfilment, and indeed no sort of guarantee of its truth. Now Christ has shown us what the Son of Man is in the purpose of God, has shown us the divine possibilities of our own nature (you, my dear Henry, will not refuse that phrase), and has shown us them in the actual circumstances of a historic life, thus revealing the road to fulfilment at which hardly any before Him had dared to guess. Jeremiah and the later Isaiah had pointed to the redemptive worth of suffering and held out the hope that Israel exiled, afflicted, forsaken might by this very experience of sin-bearing fulfil a work of vicarious sacrifice and give its life a ransom for many: their words remained an imagination until Jesus took the mission upon Himself and by the event proved it to be true. The Book of Job had hinted that the only solution of the problem of evil is in the restored and abiding experience of communion with God: this Jesus had expressed in its concrete embodiment in Himself, thereby transforming what to the author or editor of Job seemed quite unsatisfying into an evidently triumphant vindication of God's way. He had illustrated and fulfilled God's plan, and thus invited us to understand and to share it. With this invitation, life could never again be the same.

Moreover, for those who have responded, and so have gained experience of what He has done and can do, there is a still greater and more dynamic newness of life. As they follow the example of the Christ, they are not indeed thereby made perfect. Like the Apostle, at their best they can only say, "Not that I have already attained or am already made perfect, but I press on" (Phil. iii. 11, 12). But though they still fail and sin, though at times the whole effort seems Sisyphean, though on occasion they are tempted to cry, "Depart from me; for I am a sinful man, O Lord," yet in the core of their being, when temptation has done its worst with them and proved them weak and wicked, there is still something that protests, still a stronghold that refuses to surrender. "So for me with the mind I serve the law of God, even if with the flesh I serve the law of sin" (Rom. vii. 25). This had been the Apostle's conclusion; and he had affirmed it, not as a confession of defeat, but as a proclamation of victory. There was that in him which was now unconquerable; and in the strength of it he could continue the conflict with fortitude. For if, as our experience surely betokens, we die daily, yet there is in us a life immortal, a life which daily rises from the dead. "The love of Christ holds us fast."

This is what Christ has done; and the more we enter into the business of our discipleship, the more we shall acclaim its uniqueness and its sufficiency. "I ask not that thou shouldest take them out of the world"—it is not new heavens and a new earth, not Nirvana nor the Rose of Heaven that he offers to us—"but that thou shouldest keep them from the evil one"—from that permanent acquiescence in defeat, that helpless estrangement from God, that total involvement in our own self-interest which is the only real death. So the Fourth Evangelist, truest interpreter of St. Paul and of the Christian experience, expresses the purport of it (John xvii. 15). And the result is all that the saints have declared.

Or so at least it seems to one who has no competence to judge of matters too high for him. It speaks, as I have said, to my condition. For while I dare not say that I have "pressed on," while indeed at times it merely seems as if the years added sin to sin, yet if I am now much more conscious than formerly of the extent and shame of my failure, at least I am more sure of the fact and of the significance of Christ. If I cannot point to anything in myself except that He has kept me from total despair, at least I have seen in others the authentic and indisputable evidence of His victory. I have seen in them what happens to the Christian who accepts the work of Christ and enables its accomplishment; and I know that for such there is indeed "a death unto sin and a new birth unto righteousness."

But you know this far better than I—and will, I fear, be disappointed rather than encouraged by the fact that one who ought to have seen so much more has to confess so pitiable a failure. For this which I know, and for those "presumptuous sins" of which I am still unconscious, I can only beg your forgiveness.

And perhaps this one thing may be added. In the past four years—since friends and work and hopes went to smash in the cataclysm of war—there has hardly been a single night during which I have not spent at least an hour, generally between 3 and 4 a.m., in hell. That is no figure of speech, if hell means a consciousness of total estrangement from God, of utter dereliction, in which one's eyes are open to the vast selfishness and consequent hurtfulness of one's life, to the multitude of opportunities misused, loyalties betrayed and relationships perverted. Night after night, facing the fact of evil, I was quite unable to see any sign of deliverance from it—until at last, my dear Henry, came the knowledge that thus to be aware of it, thus to be tormented by it, was in itself a proof of release from it. Not to be unaware, not to be wholly absorbed and complacent, this was to have in some measure at least the possibility and indeed the fact of freedom. On the ground that I acknowledge my sin, I can make access to my God.

Yours ever
CHARLES

VII

THE HEALTH OF MAN

"I thank God through Jesus Christ." Rom. vii. 25

MY DEAR HENRY,

The new world for us Christians is not a fancy or a futurity, but a fact. For it is the old world in Christ; the old world as in our moments of communion we see it; the old world afire with the unveiled Shechinah of His presence. It is this transfigured earth, as Arthur Clutton-Brock taught my generation in his great book, *What is the Kingdom of Heaven?*, which is the world of the Second Advent, the "Realm of Ends," the *Una Sancta* and the *Communio Sanctorum*. It has no frontiers, save those of man's devising; nor any conditions of entry save those of the need which desires forgiveness and the humility which forgives; nor any "privileged citizens," since God's sun shines upon all alike; nor any official hierarchy save that which consists in service. It is in fact, as St. Paul came to see, the body of Christ, His hands and feet and ears and eyes and voice; and its membership is determined by its functioning. No man, be he pope or charcoal-burner, has the right to pronounce who are or are not of "the body": "Judge not" is surely an absolute prohibition, since it states a self-evident fact that no human being can know the secrets of his neighbour. No man, as I have already argued, may affirm his own place in the body without grave peril to his soul; and all of us will, I believe, do well to claim a place in it for all those in whose lives are the fruit of the Spirit "love, joy, peace, long-suffering, gentleness, goodness, faith, meekness, temperance" (Gal. v. 22, 23). And yet did not a young parson, fresh from his theological college and with the "Grace of Orders" presumably strong upon him, have the effrontery to tell one of my men, older, abler, and (I think) not less Christian, that "outside the Church there was no salvation," that the Church consisted only of the baptised, confirmed and validly communicating, and that he, as none of these things, was therefore outside salvation?

It is surely a pity that in the course of its history the Church has so often been identified with one or other of the three types of secular society whose characteristic activities Jesus rejected at His Temptation. There were, as you know, in the Roman world into which Christianity came, three such types, corresponding roughly to the three chief human needs, economic, religious and political. If we are to understand the nature of the Christian community, it is well first of all to look at these.

First there was, then as now, the Friendly Society, the club or guild whose purpose was the provision of benefits, treatment in illness, maintenance in old age, a funeral after death. That the Church was at one time reckoned and perhaps even registered as such a society is probable; that it borrowed from their example the system of relief which was at first the chief function of the bishop and which gave him his prestige, has been argued and is not improbable. With my own affection for the Oddfellows and my memory of the Lodge in which I passed through the offices, I can only say that even to-day a good Lodge seems to me much more like the Early Church than many of our professedly ecclesiastical gatherings. But for all that, "man does not live by bread alone": the Church is not a benefit-society: and though the physical wellbeing, the security and relief, of the brethren is a plain obligation, it is not the primary task or motive of the Church's life.

Alongside the societies for physical benefit were the priesthoods and religious orders connected with one or other of the gods and lords of the ancient pantheon. Sacred trees and wells, shrines and temples, "haunts of ancient dread" and cults newly imported from the East had each its organised body of hierophants, its priests to offer the sacrifice, its deacons to serve the altar, its acolytes to adorn the processions, its patrons to pay the bills. Wonder and worship are a normal human need and the provision of opportunities for its satisfaction is a legitimate human activity. It was an appeal to this need that Satan offered to Jesus when he bade Him fling Himself from the pinnacle and appear as the expected Messiah descending on the clouds of heaven into the Temple courts. And Jesus refused to exploit God, to impose upon man's craving for the supernatural, to satisfy his spiritual nature as a primary obligation. And yet how soon after the Apostolic Age was ended did not the Church equip itself with priests and transform the Eucharist into a sacrifice, and adopt all the hierarchy of ministrants in sacred things? And I suppose that to-day, if the ordinary man were asked what was the function of the Church, he would associate it with the upkeep of cathedrals and the providing of opportunities for worship—activities no doubt valuable and perhaps even necessary, but no more to be taken as primary than the provision of physical benefits.

Finally, there were, of course, all the manifold groupings, local, provincial, imperial, which had to do with citizenship and the rule and governance of mankind. To the Jews political independence had been so long bound up with their religion and was so plain a present objective as to make our modern distinction between sacred and secular obscure and negligible. They would never have accepted Gallio's easy distinction between ethics ("a matter of wrong-doing or wicked villainy") and religion ("words and names and your law," Acts xviii. 14, 15); and in Palestine under the Roman yoke were likely to test any prophet by his readiness to proclaim a *jehad*. So "the kingdoms of the earth and the glory of them," the establishment of a theocracy like that of Solomon or of Hildebrand, was a legitimate objective for any claimant to Messiahship, and has been the most effective if not the most subtle of temptations to ecclesiastics ever since. Power, more, I suppose, than comfort or applause, power and the ambition that accompanies it, is still "the last infirmity of noble minds." Jesus regarded it as involving an apostasy. Yet the so-called successor of St. Peter still assumes the triple crown as King of kings; and no doubt the ordering of men's lives and the maintenance of a just and stable government cannot be a matter of indifference either to the Church or to the individual Christian. I at least repudiate whole-heartedly the claim of some of my Lutheran friends that under present circumstances the Christian must take no part in political life, and am strongly opposed to disestablishment if it involves the secularising of the State. I rejoice whole-heartedly that our Archbishops are speaking out so plainly about social evils, and believe that by so doing they will do much to break down the barrier between man's two greatest and inseparable interests, his concern with God, which is religion, and with his fellows, which is politics. Nevertheless, Jesus refused this third method and type of society not less definitely than the other two.

What, then, is the Church if it is not primarily an economic, religious or political organisation? Is it an organisation at all? Or is the whole idea of a Christian community as opposed to a number of individual Christians a mistake?

We have been following St. Paul's exposition of the Gospel and the first half of the eighth chapter of Romans gives us a clear insight into his thought.

He begins with his master-motif, the indwelling of the life and mind of Christ in the believer. This is how man is freed from sin—because as Christ fills his life there is no room for sin and no interest in it. Sin is squeezed out; and its place is taken by the Spirit of holiness, which is the Spirit of Christ and the Spirit of God. The passage is, of course, a *locus classicus* for the whole doctrine of the Holy Spirit in the New Testament, though in fact here as elsewhere St. Paul is not dealing with doctrine or formal theology, but with experience. Here rooted in experience is the concept from which spring his utterances as to the nexus between Christ and His disciples and the integration of each of them with the rest, and the foundation upon which is based his whole teaching of the body of Christ.

He contends, first, that Christ's indwelling is accomplished by the imparting and receiving of His Spirit. How far the word "spirit" had for him a physical or quasi-physical meaning is wholly unimportant. In any case the gift was real and concrete—a new experience, a new outlook and mind, a new principle of life. And this Spirit was of God, literally and explicitly divine, and therefore legitimately identified with the Spirit which brooded over the waters in Genesis (i. 2), which inspired Bezaleel the craftsman and Samson the hero (Exod. xxxi. 3; Judges xiv. 6, 12) and which "spake by the prophets." Now, as embodied and therefore interpreted in Christ, the character and activities of the Spirit are plainly seen—although in certain passages of the Acts and in certain parts of the Early Church psychic excitements quite strange to the life of Jesus are given a dangerous emphasis. Yet "He shall take of mine, and shall declare it unto you" (John xvi. 14) is a true witness and test: the Spirit in us continues and fulfils the work of Christ, and the fidelity of our response and the consequent extent of His indwelling can only be appreciated by the degree to which, thus inspired, the Church resembles its Lord. Here as elsewhere the test is that of fruits: "not every one that saith unto Me Lord, Lord . . . but he that doeth the will of My Father" (Matt. vii. 21), and that will is the Spirit.

Similarly, those in whom the Spirit dwells are thereby linked not only with God in Christ, but with one another. The concept of the organic unity of believers is an inevitable consequence of belief in their individual inspiration. There can be no such thing as a solitary disciple, for in accepting Christ the believer enters into a life already widely shared: he not only shares a common loyalty, but one and the same Spirit dwells in the whole society. It is, I believe, a fact of universal experience that any deep awareness of God is accompanied by a sense of sympathy—indeed, of unity—with mankind. The love of God and the love of the brethren are indissoluble. And the reason for this is plain. There is in us all a common life, even as by our creation we have a common origin: we are literally akin. As our consciousness of God is aroused and we become sensitive to Him, we discover His presence in nature and in mankind; and recognise that we are "of one blood." When this experience is deepened and clarified by the acknowledgment of God in Christ, the vague sense of a common and permeating life is quickened into a "family feeling" as of those who share one home and are indeed brothers and sisters. The Spirit of Christ the Son is the Spirit of our adoption as sons "whereby we cry, *Abba*, Father" (Rom. viii. 15).

This concept of the Church as the family of God takes up one of the deepest and earliest thoughts of the Old Testament. Israel, if it had been a nation and a church, had primarily been so because of its organic connection with its God: He had been the Father of His people, and they had been in a special and intimate sense His children. The concept had been a naïve one—bound up with the primitive sense of the local and physical relationships between the God and His territory. It had faded with the growth of transcendentalism and the reverence that accompanies it. As the gulf widened between Him and His people, rule and ritual on their side and a host of angels and mediators on His, intervene between the parties; and the covenant loses its intimate and homely quality. But it was Christ's task to reaffirm in new and mature form these intuitions of the childhood of mankind, and to re-establish the blood relationship of the Father and His family.

Out of this blood relationship springs the developed Pauline doctrine of the Church, as the symbol of Christ in the world, as the instrument through which He works, as the body in which He comes to us in a real and continuous

Second Advent. "Second" is indeed a misleading term: for there is an absolute continuity between His presence in His physical body and His presence by His Spirit in the body of believers. Each is by its very nature the medium expressive of His life, responsive to His will, organic in the sense that its link with Him is that of living flesh and blood with the self which animates and sustains it. Between the body born of Mary and crucified under Pontius Pilate and the body which is His Church there is not merely an analogy, but an identity of function and of relatedness. Each of them has as its characteristic the fulfilment of His work in the world.

If this is the nature of the Church, if the "last things" are fulfilled in it and the Kingdom of God manifest, then the claims made on its behalf even by the most impassioned of Catholic devotees will not seem exaggerated—will, in fact, fall short of its deserts. If any earthly society could make good its calling by actually fulfilling the work of Christ, then in it the new age would be manifest, and exclusive demands (supposing—which is absurd—that such a body could make them) would be easy to justify. Mankind is so constituted that if such a body appeared it would either worship or crucify: it would not remain apathetic and mildly contemptuous. It is unnecessary to repeat what has already been treated or to argue that the all too human organisations and institutions which now represent the Church which is His body are chiefly remarkable to the ordinary man for the contrast which they present to their Master. We have sinned: only on that basis of common penitence can we face the situation that awaits us.

It may be that at that point we can meet—on the basis of our common sin and our common need. Perhaps, my dear Henry, all this talk about total depravity (a doctrine which is surely a "damnable heresy" and as preached too often only a counsel of despair) may mean that we are more ready to repent; and may even prepare the way for us to do so. I should be more convinced of this, I confess, if I saw more humility and less self-righteousness in these modern Augustinians. But even so, their Jeremiads may be used by God.

Only—and this is I think necessary—if it is the true change of heart which having seen the glory of God then recognises that it is standing on holy ground in dirty shoes, it will be penitence all round. We shall acknowledge that we have altogether gone out of the way and are altogether become abominable. We shall strip ourselves of our defences, even of the armour of traditional orthodoxy or modern scholarship wherein we have trusted. We shall include it all under one great confession of sin, one great and agonising petition for forgiveness. We shall keep back no part of the price of our self-respect. For we shall not be thinking of ourselves or the impression we wish to create, of our past and its distinctions or of our future and its uncertainties. We shall be thinking of God in Christ, and His Spirit and His body.

And if that can happen in us, it can also happen, is perhaps even now happening, in others. Indeed, out of our own knowledge we are sure that it is so. Faced with a position intolerably tragic when all our dreams of human welfare or individual service have been shattered, there is for all of us a call which surely even the least imaginative can hardly ignore. To forget our shibboleths, to realise that our boasted infallibilities and disciplines, our traditions and movements, our Catholicisms and Protestantisms have led us into this horror, and to confess that in our tithing of mint and cummin, our compassing of heaven and earth for proselytes, our delight in vestments and titles of respect we have played the hypocrite and become children of hell and devourers of widows' houses—can we make a beginning here, applying the cap where it fits, but making no excuses, since if we are less guilty in one respect we are very certainly more so in another?

"As many as are led by the Spirit of God, these are the

sons of God." So the Apostle declared; and he had been a Pharisee. He knew what it was to have been brought up in the strictest sect, to have had a brilliant career, to have been marked out for high preferment, to have companied with the great. If any man might boast and claim privilege, he more; and he speaks of what he has had to surrender with a passion that reveals how much it has cost. Yet Christ had received it—the holocaust of Saul of Tarsus: and out of it had sprung phoenix-like the winged messenger who had carried the fiery cross from east to west and set the world ablaze.

He had done it, humanly speaking, by a combination of qualities neither of them rare, but usually mutually exclusive —a concentrated passion for Christ amounting almost to the absorption of a fanatic, and a versatility, an ingenuity, a mastery of means which enabled him to take advantage of every opening and wrestle with every obstacle until at last the stubborn obduracy of events became plastic, a road was found through the barriers, and the very circumstances which limited his course became opportunities for further service. He never despaired of his objective, of the Christ to whom he was dedicated; and he never assumed that any-one, however alien to him as a pious Jew, was outside the reach, or unresponsive to the appeal, of Christ's Spirit.

The secret of his double equipment and therefore of his amazing impact upon history is easy to understand. His con-version had transformed a man of brilliant parts, a man distracted by unsatisfied desires and wasting his life over feverish efforts to which his own ambition and his loyalty to his religion alternately urged him, into a man of integrated character, of wide and co-ordinated interests, and therefore of almost limitless efficacy. His love of Christ was too rich in content, too free from any taint of possessiveness, too wholehearted and complete to become exclusive or distort-ing. His versatility, linked with his devotion, became a harmony of co-operating aptitudes, a pattern to which every fibre of his being could contribute. His varied experience as native of Tarsus, pupil of Gamaliel and citizen of Rome gave him points of contact with all the world of his own day. His restless energy, saved by its singleness of purpose from fussiness and wastage, sustained him through labours almost superhuman. More than any man in history, he combined the qualities of strategist and of tactician and deserves the title of "the dreamer whose dreams came true." Few men have suffered more from the exaggerations of commentators: "Paulinism" is in general a monstrous substitute for his gospel. None have been, in recent times, more denounced or more caricatured. But his achievement stands—a permanent and splendid witness to what the Spirit of Christ can do when it takes free possession of a disciple.

There is a scene, one of the few scenes in the New Testament in which the story deals with a personage of the "great world," the scene at Corinth when Paul appeared before Gallio. The proconsul of Achaia, brother to the great Stoic saint and thinker, Seneca, and himself a man of charm, of philosophy, of character, may well stand as typical of that scientific humanism which then as now so largely represented "the opinion of all educated men." His prisoner, brought up in the birthplace of Stoicism and certainly familiar with some at least of its masterpieces, shared his sense of duty, his respect for law, his moral integrity. But, unlike Gallio, his life was centred not in a disciplined self-sufficiency, but in a self-emptying devotion. Gallio's utterance, typical of his outlook, reveals the sharp contrast between them when he dismisses religion and Christ as "words and names." Between the two of them, as between humanism and Christianity, the issue has been decided by history. If ever humanism could have fulfilled its claims, it was surely in the century which began with Seneca and ended with Marcus Aurelius, when all that was best in it had imperial power and unlimited opportunity. Yet it was Christ who prevailed. Gallio has become a name synonymous with carelessness and flippancy; Seneca, having narrowly escaped canonisation as a supposed convert of St. Paul, has fallen into oblivion; and Marcus Aurelius has (or had till recently) his *Meditations* bound in lambskin as pretty gifts for adolescent agnostics at Christmas.

Yet if the Spirit which St. Paul proclaimed had prevailed, this contrast between humanist and Christian would surely have been done away. Certainly the Apostle was ready to take the Stoic virtues as common ground and to recognise that so far he and they stood for a common cause. Indeed, in some of his utterances—for example, his references to the civil power (e.g. Rom. xiii. 1, 4: "he is a minister of God to thee for good")—he is evidently prepared to recognise the fruit of the Spirit in these very Stoics; and to make his approach to them as to men already in some sense within the family. If that method had been pursued, if the Church had not been driven by persecution into revilings and exclusiveness, if the glow and generosity and vital power of the Christian community had been maintained and made accessible to Gallio and his kind, the marvellous advance of the gospel from Calvary to Cæsar's palace in one generation might not have been checked.

For there is that in the quality of New Testament religion which grips and fascinates even while it searches and judges. The documents enshrining it, these casual letters of St. Paul and others, these collections of records about Jesus and His followers, have not survived without reason. They do not owe their survival to the power and persistence of the Church; for without them the Church would long ago have fallen into superstition and decay; and they alone have enabled its constant revival and reform. They live because of the sheer vitality, the passion and divinity, that is in them. They live because they embody the Spirit of Christ and testify to His works. No one reading them with attention and sensitiveness can fail to see that what distinguished the Christians corporately and individually in those early days was not the character of their creed, nor the purity of their morals; still less was it their *cultus* or their hierarchy. It was the conscious indwelling of the Spirit, the discovery of love and joy and peace and fortitude as the Spirit's authentic fruit, and the readiness, therefore, recognising the Spirit's presence, to claim kinship with "all that was true, and reverent, and just, and pure, and lovable, and of good report" (Phil. iv. 8).

For this surely is the cause of the thankfulness that rings through the whole New Testament: the Kingdom has come, and in Christ is already established: the new heaven and the new earth of which prophets, Hebrew and pagan, have spoken is now an accomplished fact; and we are in it. That in spite of this we have still to wrestle and agonise, are still sin-stained and often defeated is, as we have seen, not finally irreconcilable with our faith. Indeed, from our experience we learn (or ought to learn) this plain lesson, that if we doubt the presence of the Kingdom and wish to work for its future appearing, the way to do so is simply to behave as if it were already here. This is the secret. The Kingdom has come; for the Kingdom is the Spirit of the living Christ. The Kingdom has come; and it is our business to live in it. Our repentance is, as the first public utterance of Jesus declared, that we believe the good news.

We are indeed, my dear Henry, living in "the last things," in the realm of ends; for to us means and ends are one and the same, the practice of the presence of God in His gracious gift of Christ and in the fellowship of His Spirit. This is our "eternal now"; and there are (I think) no conditions for its realisation except Christ's one word, "Only believe," and that other which is in fact identical with it, "Forgive and ye shall be forgiven."

Yours ever

CHARLES

VIII

THE PURPOSE OF GOD

"Unto the glorious liberty of the children of God." Rom. viii. 21

M<small>Y DEAR</small> H<small>ENRY</small>,
 It is, of course, very nice to say, "Live eternally," "Believe that you are in heaven and behave accordingly, and you'll find that it works," but at present earth looks much more like hell, and for many of us, vast multitudes of folk in hospitals and concentration camps, in battle or in suspense, every minute is an agony. A small and mystically gifted minority may be able to practise the presence of Christ in a tank or a submarine or a bomber; a small and privileged few may be able to find a monastery and shut themselves away from the mess. But most of us——!

I don't want to dispute it—though for my own part I have never before or since been so constantly aware of God, so constantly "accompanied" as during the nine months that I was under fire with the Second Division in 1917–18. Nor do I believe that the power-house will be found in a place of prayer in California or a hermit's cave in the Himalayas: power will come out of the furnace where men walk with the Son of God.

But the objection remains and we must face it. Is this Christian gospel addressed only to individuals, to an elect who through temperament or circumstances have the opportunity to accept it? Christians from St. Augustine to Dean Inge have so interpreted it; and, as we all know, if there are universalist texts and probabilities in the New Testament, there are also warnings of a terrific and almost Calvinistic austerity. What are we to say to the man who says, "Thanks very much for your, or God's, offer. It must be nice to be able to accept it and know that you are saved. You can afford it—perhaps! I can't, and, to be honest, don't want to." If said in scorn and self-satisfaction, that sort of remark need not much matter—except to set us asking whether we deserve it. It is not seldom said by people, genuine, humble-minded, anxious to serve, but wholly unable to reconcile the claims of the Gospel with the facts of life, and therefore unwilling and rightly unwilling to accept dope or to encourage hypocrisy.

It seems to me that it is with these folks in mind that St. Paul turns from his scheme of salvation to the new argument that fills the last half of the eighth chapter, and is perhaps the most remarkable passage that he ever wrote. It looks as if he had suddenly said to himself, "Yes. So far so good. In my own experience of myself and of others, Christ has done what I've described, set men free from evil, and bound them together in a community of service. But is this just a fact to be declared and advocated? Or is it of wider significance? Does it contain an explanation of the whole riddle of life? Is it a clue to a *Weltanschauung*, such as all of us need and could share?"

So he plunges into his interpretation of the purpose of God in the whole sphere of nature and history.

There is, there must be, a meaning in the universe; and Christ must give a fresh significance to that meaning. For in Christ something new and illuminative has happened. History could never be to the Jew merely the random revolution of a kaleidoscope, the permutations of a fixed number of created things. For although God had ended His works on the sixth day, He had surely resumed them "like a giant refreshed" on the eighth. For He was a living God, a God who works, the God who ceaselessly strove with His people. History, therefore, as the record of His works, is still going on. It is incomplete; it is still in the making; and in it there is progress, up to and including and proceeding from Christ. This is his first thesis. St. Paul sees it, naturally, in terms of the stories in Genesis "the creation was made subject to frustration, not through any will of its own, but by the immediate act of God who made it subject" (Rom. viii. 20).

The creative process has not reached its goal in one leap: it is indeed so conditioned that it could not do so: there is "a race to be run not without dust and sweat":

> "*a battle's to fight ere the guerdon be gained*
> *The reward of it all.*"

And as old Socrates had put it, the "game is worth the playing and our hope is great." The end is not yet.

The process is incomplete, but it is pregnant. That is the character of its pain. "We know well that the whole creation groans together and travails together until this hour: nay, more, we ourselves who have the foretaste of the Spirit, we ourselves groan within ourselves, awaiting our adoption" (Rom. viii. 22, 23). The process is one of eager expectation. Nature, like a young wife waiting for her firstborn, makes ready for the coming of the child that is to be. When the days are complete, God's family will be born upon the earth. In their manifestation the agony of the ages will find its fulfilment and its justification.

Having laid down this second thesis, the Apostle rises to a new and more splendid theme. It is not enough to see the story of the universe as the drama of the birth of the children of God. Indeed, to regard it so may be false to the nature of God himself. He is not as the gods of the heathen "careless of mankind," not an Olympian spectator watching the acts of the play and rewarding its performers with His applause. He is himself involved, a partner in the effort, a sharer in the agony. His Spirit gives aid to our infirmity: "the very Spirit comes in alongside of us with groanings unuttered" (Rom. viii. 26). It is as an actor, not a spectator, that God takes His part in the drama. We in our weakness and our pain are not alone; are not the sport of blind forces uncontrolled and perhaps uncontrollable; are accompanied, sustained, encouraged.

Therefore (and so he comes to his fourth and final thesis), the end is sure: "we know well that God makes everything work together for good to them that love him" (Rom. viii. 28). We cannot see His plan; we cannot tell why He thus chooses us for Himself; we very certainly have no merit that deserves and no piety that cajoles His favour. He has chosen us; and we accept His act. And therefore we need not be afraid. A relationship has come into being, a purpose is being fulfilled, which nothing can destroy or foreclose. We are held by the love of Christ whatever befall us upon earth. In that love the weakest of us is a conqueror. From that love neither death nor life nor things present nor things to come shall ever have power to separate us.

It is a superb passage; one of those outbreaks of sheer inspiration into which from time to time the Apostle is lifted. In a sense, like the hymn to love in 1 Cor. xiii, it is a thing apart: yet in fact it springs from and consummates what has gone before. For the grand sweep of the process which culminates in the manifestation of the sons of God implies and is worked out by the repetition in each individual of that redemptive work whereby the body of each is delivered from corruption and which is for each his adoption. He has described this redemption previously, in the great confession of Chapter VII. Here he does not repeat it nor amplify his reference to the coming of the Son of God. But enough is said to make it abundantly plain that his thought is wholly realistic and wholly consistent with the later passages, for example, in Eph. iv, in which the subject is fully expounded. Here is no apocalyptic fantasy, no demand for miracle or "divine irruption." The process is as natural as childbirth, as wholesome and as human as the hope of Israel—of which it is in fact the fulfilment now made possible in Christ.

It is a superb passage. Based, of course, upon the imagery of the ancient folk-lore of the Jews, it lifts their intuition on to a plane appropriate to the outlook of the modern mind so that its thought becomes compatible with our own concepts of an agelong evolution and a vast cosmic urge. Here is no

97

such failure to grasp the notion of progress as recent shallow minds have attributed at random to the peoples of the ancient world. Here is no doctrine of a Devil able to pervert God's good purpose, nor of any total depravity of nature and man. Here is no excuse for the dark subtleties of the doctrine of election and those grim verdicts upon the reprobate with which "Paulinism" has so largely been concerned. Here is such a picture of the love and sufficiency of God as is the authentic flowering of the "root of Jesse," the firm foundation for a Christian and incarnational philosophy.

Why, then, has such an utterance, placed at so obvious a climax in the greatest of Pauline Epistles, and manifestly declaring a master's exposition of his subject, been so generally ignored? Why, in these days of emergent evolution, is its message proclaimed so diffidently, and by so few? The answer reveals one of the chief—indeed, I believe the very chiefest—defects of our Christianity.

The fault was not due to the Early Church. The first adequate theology, still perhaps the noblest ever formulated, the Logos theology of the Greek Apologists, which had its fullest expression in the Christian Platonism of Clement of Alexandria and Origen, did full justice to it. Justin, when he allows to Greek philosophy a place parallel to that of the Mosaic Law in the revelation of God and so can call Heracleitus and Socrates, not less than Abraham, Christians before Christ; Clement, when he treats all human history as the record of the education of mankind by the Divine Word and a preparation, "at diverse times and sundry manners," but continuously, for the coming of that Word in fullness in Christ; Origen, when he devotes the concentrated passion of his life and the vast and versatile gifts of his genius to the interpretation of the same theme, seeking to make every element of human knowledge contribute to the building up of a worthy theology, and regarding the whole universe as the expression of a divine process of self-manifestation; these lifted the thought of

St. Paul on to a place of eminence among the great philosophies of mankind. It is one of the tragedies of history that the work of this brilliant succession of Christian thinkers was allowed not merely to come to an end, but to fall into neglect, oblivion and condemnation. If we are to handle effectively the task of elucidating a Christian theology for the twentieth century, we must, I think, ignore all the elaborate structures of later orthodoxy, Catholic and Protestant, which for to-day are literally irrelevant, and return to the point at which Origen was removed. There is much in his work and something in that of his predecessors that will need drastic correction; for the method of allegorising which they applied to Scripture is impossible for us as it was misleading for them. But the main lines of their concept of God's purpose in the universe are of permanent value and to-day of paramount significance.

It is easy enough to pick holes in the work of the Christian Platonists, though much of the scorn poured upon them is based on gross exaggerations and false antitheses. It is not true that they had no sense of sin: Clement denounces the vices and foibles of his day as fervently as any Puritan of the Commonwealth. It is not true that they do not preach redemption: Origen, even if he dares to believe that in the end all men will be saved, has a passion for souls as strong as any revivalist. Nor is it just to accuse them of an over-emphasised intellectualism: they were scholars, but by no means pedants, and their interest was as much in the love of God as in the knowledge of Him. Nor, finally, is their doctrine fully described when we have labelled it "Binitarian": if it is liable to suggest an unknown God represented in the universe by His Word and so to approximate to Jewish or even pagan deism, this is not a defect necessarily inherent in their scheme of thought and is in fact a point against which both the great Alexandrians are constantly on guard.

Rather their work is weak as we have suggested, because

of the handicap of its method of exegesis. The allegorical method of interpretation, though derived from belief in the truth of the documents and devised as a means to protect that truth, nevertheless effectively emptied them of historical worth. The record of events became nothing but a book of elaborate enigmas, to be interpreted by the ingenuity and applied at the discretion of the teacher. In consequence mythology took the place of verifiable fact; Christ became a kind of theosophist; and the element of speculation and esotericism became gravely overstressed. Origen, by his devotion to the Bible, did much to counteract this tendency. But only a radical revision of method, only the discovery of the true principles of historical criticism could do full justice to their subject.

But this theology possessed the one thing necessary, a full and proportionate concept of God's nature and work. It had, what no subsequent age has yet recovered, a real doctrine of the continuity and energy of God's working in the world—that is, a worthy theology of the Holy Spirit. Clement may have assigned to the *Logos* the functions of the Spirit: Origen may have failed to discriminate clearly between the functions of the Second and the Third Persons of the Trinity: but both of them had the root of the matter in their lives and in their thought. For them the constant, vitalising activity of God at work in His world was the essential element of their teaching. It is infinitely regrettable that the lines which they laid down so well were never followed.

For, in the age of formulation and incessant controversies that ensued, the proportion of the faith was destroyed—and thereby most of its vitality was dissipated. In the great credal system hammered out by the Councils and expounded in the literature of the period full justice was done to God's works in the past: He had created the world; His Son had come down from Heaven to redeem it and would come again to judge it. But of His present indwelling life, of His age-long purpose, and of the splendid conditions and hope of its fulfilment there was not a word. Christianity, which had been a creative and victorious adventure, fragrant with the gay courage of the catacombs and the high chivalry of the martyrs, now became little more than a mummified relic of its former self, fit only for the mausoleum of the monasteries and the museum of the cathedrals.

Put it otherwise. The doctrine of Christ, the teaching about His work and meaning, had been shorn of all that rich and manifold content which had been associated with Him by St. Paul and expressed in His title, *Logos*. He was now little more than the divine Son of Mary whose present function was limited to occupying a throne in Heaven and allowing His Body and Blood to be offered as a daily sacrifice on the altars of His Church. Nor had the functions of the *Logos* as the creative energy in nature and history and the divine and educative reason in men been transferred, as they should surely have been, to the Holy Spirit. That great name, in some sense the centre and theme of Apostolic Christianity, was now a *nomen nudum*, a word without content, a formula in prayers, a clause, but a bare clause, in the Creed of Nicea. When later in the century the Spirit had been granted consubstantial deity with Father and Son in the Trinity of the orthodox, this status had been settled merely by analogy; His meaning and functions, His relation to nature and history and the lives of men were never seriously discussed, and if the words "the Lord, the life-giver, who spake by the prophets" were added to the Creed, the general description of His activity given by the Fathers is simply the bald and mystifying statement that "He proceeds." The Spirit became in fact little more than a convenient and impressive term for the magical powers bestowed by God upon the hierarchy and available with the appropriate ritual for their use. And do you think, my dear Henry, that the vast majority of our Church-people have any very different notion to-day?

I don't believe they have. If one could look into their

minds when they respond, "Take not Thy Holy Spirit from us," would they, or for that matter the authors of the phrase, be able to give it any clear meaning? Doves, flames, seven-fold gifts which no one has ever classified intelligibly, gifts bestowed by episcopal hands—what sort of teaching does our Church give to interpret this medley of symbols? If we are honest, would not most of us have to confess that we are precisely in the position of those twelve whom St. Paul found at Ephesus (Acts xix. 1–12), who did not so much as know if there was any Holy Ghost? And in consequence all this glorious knowledge that the whole creative process is the scene of His energy, that every least impulse towards fullness of life is linked up at every level with His majestic effort, that in us all wherever men and women are loving and joyous and peaceful and brave He is manifested, and that all our aspirations towards a truer brotherhood, a nobler community, of mankind are acknowledgments of His leading—all this finds no place in the worship and witness of our Church.

Nor is it any excrescence or insignificance in our Christian faith that we are thus ignoring. It is in some sense the very keystone of the arch of doctrine that binds together all the rest into a solid structure. If the doctrine of the Holy Spirit be ignored, the doctrine of creation becomes merely the tale of a bit of carpentry, of a world knocked together by a craftsman out of material external to himself, and then left to run by itself; incarnation becomes a theophany, for if incarnation has no relation to inspiration and the indwelling work of the Spirit, then not only is the Creed ("conceived by the Holy Ghost") meaningless, but all possibility of interpreting or imitating Christ becomes absurd; and atone-ment becomes magic, for it is only as by the operation of the Spirit working in us we are made at one with the mind of Christ that the word has any realistic meaning. The doctrine is essential. We have mislaid and neglected it. We must repent.

If the doctrine is essential, still more so is the experience.

No one can study the literature of the New Testament or reflect upon the quality of the Apostolic Church without feeling that in both there is disclosed a remarkable and indeed unique vitality, a life and life abundant such as mankind has always desired, but never elsewhere attained. These people, these little groups of slaves and petty tradesmen, the flotsam and jetsam of the Levant, are alive, supercharged with sensitiveness and passion and energy, dynamic because integrated and unafraid. That is why their words and deeds survive, and the years are dated from their Lord. And they are "the community of the Holy Spirit," the people to whom He was the very criterion of their existence, its source and sustenance. All through Acts and Epistles it is assumed that these "believers" have some mark upon them, some power with them, that sets them apart from others and makes their days a wonder and a joy. It is "the power of the Holy Spirit," a power reasonable, realistic, revolutionary, a power that can make them and all things new. And we only know it, if at all, by hearsay and at second hand!

There then, my dear Henry, is our task—as I see it and have seen it for years. To discover or recover the secret of Pentecost, the experience of life "in the Spirit" and the outlook upon the universe which that life involves.

Eighteen years ago I made a first attempt at such a recovery. I was in Liverpool with a bishop deeply concerned to bring unity and inspiration to his clergy in order to prepare them for evangelism. I wrote and lectured and preached on the subject continuously. Then we planned a course of studies centred upon the work of the Spirit in nature and history, in Scripture and the Church. We explored the whole field in the programme of the Church Congress held at Southport in 1926. We followed it up by the plans which led to the movement called the Way of Renewal, a movement whose object was to gather and instruct the clergy both by schools of study and by carefully prepared literature. We carried the work all over the dioceses of England. And we saw enough to be very sure that, where a living faith in the Spirit was given, great results did in fact follow.

I shall never forget those schools—for the penitence and the wonder and the joy that they brought. To see men who had lost all hope in God, for themselves and for their people; men who had fallen back from faith into reliance upon a fiercely held shibboleth, a stiff, Protestant bibliolatry or the latest little manual of Catholic practice; men moss-grown with neglect who had turned in despair to their gardens and their glebes; men who concealed the deadness of their souls beneath a hectic activity of meetings and committees; to see such men after a few days of prayer and comradeship and encouragement beginning to discover afresh their faith in God and to find that He had need of them for His great adventure, and to believe that even in Little Puddlington they could fit themselves for His service. I can never forget the beauty of it—or the sure hope that it inspired.

They took the work from me—no doubt for adequate cause. They handed it over to persons, older, more cautious, more respectable. And in a few months it was dead. Then they dressed up a changeling in its place—one of those evangelistic campaigns on the lines of the eight-day missions which have become so heavily familiar.

They killed the baby then. But the life that was in it can be re-embodied; and perhaps the time for its revival is near. At least for myself I am sure of this, that as we can enter into that vision of the creative purpose of God which came to fill and dominate the thought of St. Paul; as we can recover the passion and work for the unity of the early Christians; as we can feel and respond to "the gift of the Holy Spirit," so even now we can in our measure be used to redeem the time.

And for you and me, my dear Henry, called to serve in this great day of the Lord, this is all and this is enough—"God, and God's children and God's earth," and Christ the consummation of them all.

Yours ever

CHARLES